Approaches to Case-Study

A Handbook for Those Entering the Therapeutic Field

of related interest

Structuring the Therapeutic Process
Compromise with Chaos: The Therapist's
Response to the Individual and the Group
Murray Cox
ISBN 1 85302 028 1

Coding the Therapeutic Practice
Emblems of Encounter:
A Manual for Counsellors and Therapists
Murray Cox
ISBN 1 85302 029 X

Play Therapy
Where the Sky Meets the Underworld
Ann Cattanach
ISBN 1 85302 211 X

Art Therapy and Dramatherapy
Masks of the Soul
Sue Jennings and Åse Minde
ISBN 1 85302 027 3

Movement and Drama in Therapy
2nd edition
Audrey Wethered
Foreword by Chloë Gardner
ISBN 1 85302 199 7

The Metaphoric Body
Guide to Expressive Therapy through
Images and Archetypes
Leah Bartal and Nira Ne'eman
Foreword by Harris Chaiklin
ISBN 1 85302 152 0

Approaches to Case-Study

A Handbook for Those Entering the Therapeutic Field

Robin Higgins

Jessica Kingsley Publishers
London and Bristol, Pennsylvania

First published in the United Kingdom in 1993 by
Jessica Kingsley Publishers Ltd
116 Pentonville Road
London N1 9JB

Copyright © 1993 Robin Higgins

British Library Cataloguing in Publication Data
Higgins, Robin
Approaches to Case-Study: Handbook for
Those Entering the Therapeutic Field
I. Title
361.3

ISBN 1-85302-182-2

Printed and Bound in Great Britain by
Cromwell Press, Melksham, Wiltshire

Contents

Acknowlegements

In the preparation of this book, I am deeply grateful to Jessica Kingsley and Helen Skelton; to Daphne Hamilton-Fairley, Marietta Marcus, and Alison Feess-Higgins; to staff and students at the Laban Centre for Movement and Dance; and to colleagues and patients, without whose contributions down the years, I would have had no case-studies to approach.

Some Preliminary Questions

When we set out on a journey, it sometimes helps to have a rough map of landmarks to guide us on the way. In a case-study, these landmarks take the form of questions we may need to ask ourselves, our colleagues, our patients, and their associates.

This book is punctuated by these questions. Taken together they may be read as a provisional map or format, which may help to give a case-study structure and shape or to suggest avenues that might be worth exploring (cf. Cox 1978). The format contains many more questions than would be asked in any one case-study (let alone in any one interview). We should always be guided by the directions the interview takes over what questions may or may not be relevant, what questions we may tactfully ask.

As we gain experience, we can become more selective in the questions we ask, changing this provisional format for a different one, or even abandoning the idea of a format altogether. That is for the future.

For the moment, we should merely note that this format, this skeleton of questions on which a case-study is hung, and indeed the case-study itself, illustrate a principle we shall come upon in various guises throughout the book. Gregory Bateson outlined this principle as a phasic alternation of loose and tight thinking (Bateson 1973). Any creative act, any progress in our thought involves this capacity for successive loosening and tightening of conceptual systems. We need such systems to give us a sense of structure, yet we need constantly to dismantle and refashion them to avoid rigidity. The format of questions illustrates the shaping of the system; the selecting, changing, and omitting of questions, illustrate the re-fashioning of it. (see also Classification in Chapter VII and Phases in the growth of Research in Chapter VIII.)

The questions themselves are not meant to be fired point-blank, one after another, at the patient. Many touch on highly sensitive areas and are designed to stay in the interviewer's mind rather than to be put into spoken words. Their presence may suggest significant topics to be considered in the ripeness of time; that is, if and when the patient is ready to broach them. Here, as elsewhere, tact plays the most important part in a case-study.

Most of the questions are directed at you as the interviewer addressing the patient. 'What are the patient's views on' or 'Can you assist the patient to amplify experiences about' or 'What is your assessment of the patient's complaints, behaviour, personality...' At times, however, for example when covering personal background, the questions are directed at you yourself on the rationale that examining your own experience in these areas may offer the most constructive way into examining your patients' experience.

For the benefit of students in arts therapy training, in music, visual arts, movement or drama, additional questions bearing particularly on their field have been included. Since the arts therapies are being used increasingly in social and medical settings, it is hoped these more specialised questions may not be without interest for others such as social workers, counsellors and medical students.

The early questions we need to ask before settling down to a case-study are:

1. What am I being asked to do in this case? What is the problem and what are the possible solutions?

2. What is my role and who are my colleagues? What constitutes the system in which I play a part?

3. Why does this particular case intrigue me? Why have I selected this particular person or situation for special investigation? What is peculiar about them and about me for selecting them? What do they mean to me?

4. Am I treating the patient primarily as an example of a more general issue which preoccupies me or primarily as someone who is unique and of interest in his or her own right? Or as a bit of both? If the last, how am I resolving the uncomfortable incompatibility of case as example and case as unique?

In the lay-out of a case-study in the arts therapies, it is customary (see for example the Institute of Psychiatry's document 1982) to include sections on:

> *Social Context in which the case-study is being conducted,* for example in clinic, hospital, school, or other institution.

The Complaints or Reasons for Referral, with their immediate past history.

The Family History, including the social context of the patient's past and present life.

The Personal History, including early and subsequent development, education, career, marriage, other turning points.

Personality and Attributes, including an assessment of cognitive, emotional and imaginative capacity.

A Formulation of what is wrong (Diagnosis) and treatment plan.

Progress Notes.

A Final Formulation of what has been achieved, what remains to be done and what is likely to happen (Prognosis).

The plan of the book follows this sequence. The ultimate aim will be the integration of five 'columns':

1. The record of clinical observations including

2. Observations occurring in one or more arts media.

3. The traditional classifications of medical and psychological disorders.

4. The submission of descriptive non-experimental observations to the setting-up of hypotheses and the testing of these hypotheses for falsifiability.

5. The shaping of a case-study into a healing fiction.

CHAPTER 1

The Idiom of Case-Study (1)

Questions

1. *What is a case? What is a case-study?*

2. *What is the context in which a case-study is carried out?*

3. *What roles and relations are involved in any particular case-study? Who are the protagonists?*

4. *How does a case-study differ from biography, autobiography, a roman à clef? a myth or an archetypal plot such as Oedipus, Macbeth or Job? a single-case research study?*

The Case as the Unit of Accountability

A deep-seated law of nature is that of demand and supply. In practicing any type of therapy we cannot avoid the basic search this law poses: to define the nature of a difficulty as presented by the patient (his or her demand) in terms of ways that will assist its resolution (our supply). The unit on which this search centres is the case (for some medical applications of the law of supply and demand see Culyer 1991, Armstrong 1991, Frater and Costain 1992).

The case is the unit, the brick, with which we build our theoretical models, whether of illness and health, or of social, medical, and legal services. The case is the foundation of many human empirical studies. Our science and art arises from an accurate appreciation of the single case. The record of this appreciation lies in a case-study.

So our initial search raises the following inter-related questions:

1. What is a case?

2. What is the patient expecting or demanding in general and of the therapist in particular?

3. What can the therapist supply?

We will consider some aspects of these questions straight away. Wider implications will emerge as the book unfolds.

The Patient and the Case

Analogies to medical and social-work cases may be found in the 'briefs' and case-lore of lawyers and, more recently, in industrial or institutional case-studies, which occupy a central role in the training of managers.

In general terms a case arises when a *person (A) in a predicament calls on another person (B) for aid*. We call (A) the patient or client and (B) the professional, (nurse, doctor, therapist), i.e., someone who professes to have some training appropriate for aiding the patient in his or her predicament.

At this point, some word derivations are relevant. The English word 'case' has two root-meanings, each reaching back to a different Latin seed. The first meaning can roughly be given as 'an event or happening' and is derived from 'casus', the past participle of the Latin verb 'cadere' meaning to fall. A happening is something which 'befalls us'.

Buried in the classic meaning of 'casus' were suggestions that the 'fall' went with unexpectedness, an accident, or some stroke of misfortune. The prominence of the word 'case' in medical and legal lore, two areas dealing primarily with human suffering, preserves these classical overtones of unexpectedness and misfortune. Certainly, in selecting a case for presentation, we implicitly embark on describing somebody or something we find problematic and disturbing, somebody in a predicament himself or provoking a predicament in us, somebody or something requiring a solution.

The second meaning of the English word 'case' is 'something which contains something else': a suit-case, a book-case or a stair-case. Here the Latin root is 'capsa' meaning a repository, and stems from 'capire', that multi-purpose verb whose many meanings sprout from the idea of 'taking in hand' (cf. Italian capire, to understand). In this sense, a case-study represents the frame in which we describe and seek to contain our meeting with a predicament, the patient's and our own. This enclosure of a person's story, the setting of it in a historical and social context, not only gives it distance and dignity but in addition provides a form for the slow unfolding of a myth. This unfolding in turn, as we shall see, can have profound implications for patients, therapists, and healing alike.

The word 'patient' comes from the passive Latin verb 'patior', meaning 'I bear with or suffer'. A patient is one who bears with adverse circumstances, one who suffers in an alien situation. The term 'client', often nowadays used instead of 'patient', comes from the Indo-European root 'klei-' (meaning 'to lean, incline') through the Latin 'clinare' ('bend', 'turn') and 'cliens' (accusative 'clientem') meaning one who 'leans' or 'bends' on someone else (see further in Klein 1966). In Latin, the meaning of 'cliens' was extended to include 'being a companion', with interesting analogies for therapy (see Lewis and Short 1879).

A case, then, implies a professional relation between two people, the term 'professional' distinguishing the relation from the many others with which we are involved: relations with our families, for example, or our friends.

Patients and suffering

The sufferings of patients arise from a combination of events occurring inside and outside of them. Sometimes there is a clear outside reason for the patient's acute pain; sometimes there is none. People sometimes feel a patient ought to be suffering when he or she is not. This is perhaps particularly true of children who, because they are failing or recalcitrant in some way may be brought along to a clinic by a parent weighed down with a concern that is noticeably absent in the child.

Alternatively, a patient may appear to be registering much more distress than seems appropriate to an outsider. He or she may then be accused of putting on an act, of seeking attention or sympathy, of being hysterical or simply of malingering. Doctors and therapists are not un-known to categorise patients as 'good' or 'bad' according to how much patients voice their suffering, complain or otherwise rock the boat. But in this as in other respects, the supply side may be conveying more about its own attitude to suffering than about the attitudes of those it is supposed to be servicing. In the last resort, the degree of their suffering can only be measured by the patients themselves.

Once patients unload their suffering on to another, both parties become involved in it. Suffering is infectious. Of course the other may resist getting involved; the arts of medicine and therapy are braced with defensive ploys against being dragged down by suffering. Up to a point such ploys are part of a necessary survival kit. Clearly there is little to be gained by the supply side simply joining up with the demand. But as with all defences, what starts out as a healthy adaptation may later assume pathological forms; there are many instances in therapy where the supply side's resistance to the (suffering of) demand becomes counter-productive (see Szasz 1961, Goffman 1974 and 1984, Higgins 1963(c) also Higgins 1990).

In general, this issue of involvement in suffering, the empathy with it and the resistance to it, is at the centre of any therapeutic effort. We shall meet it repeatedly as we explore case-study. Obstacles to progress arise when we cannot understand what is going on in the suffering individuals we are seeking to treat; such obstacles disperse when we can learn from the patient (Casement 1985), that is, when we can learn constructively through the shared suffering.

The Case as Person and/or Situation

A 'case' may refer to a person (as in Freud's case-studies of Dora, Little Hans, Dr Schreber, or the Rat Man) or to a group of persons (the case of family X, the Midwich cuckoos, the Mysterious Five, the Birmingham Six). This is the word-usage of prime interest to therapists and others working in the clinical field with human problems.

The build up of a case-study through observing, examining, taking a history, and writing up the findings, entails from the start two people, patient and therapist, and the relation between them. In the resonance, interactive rhythms, and projective identification which occur between these two people, the whole issue of any isolated individual case-study becomes open to question. The forces in this patient-therapist field arise from what the patient demands (or supplies), and what the therapist supplies (or demands). These forces must clearly influence what the therapist observes and what the patient allows him to observe; what questions are asked or not asked; the mode of asking them; and what is deemed worth setting in the record or what is jettisoned, overlooked or forgotten.

The word 'case' is used in a different sense when applied to situations rather than persons. We speak of a case of 'flu, diphtheria, tuberculosis, or Aids, and our interest in such cases may have as much to do with the organism that is causing the problem as with the host who is harbouring it. We become similarly engaged in other impersonal cases: such as a case of depression, or of crime (a murder case), a case of an outstanding event (the Dreyfus case), or of a UFO (unidentified flying object), of impressionism, of terrorism, or the case of the missing link.

In applying the word 'case' to an impersonal situation, we continue to use the imagination which lies behind our involvement in the personal case, behind, that is, our attempts, to understand ourselves, other humans, and the relations between us. We retain the creative metaphors from these human fields, but transfer them to impersonal languages: the language of maths and science, or of an artistic medium such as music, painting or literature.

In a case-study, both usages of the word 'case' are relevant. The structures we employ for describing the events are themselves instances of these impersonal media. A more detailed look at two different imaginative worlds for presenting 'case-as-a-situation' is given in the last two Chapters of the book.

Some examples

1. A young man is referred to an arts therapist by a psychiatrist. The letter of referral gives the patient's age (20 years), occupation (librarian), and problem (generalised tension). It summarises his background (eldest of three, two sisters); mentions a diagnosis (anxiety state) and some prescribed medication (anxiolytic drugs). It expresses appreciation for the arts therapist's proposed contribution.

For the arts therapist who decided to write up this story, the case raised several layers of predicaments: those experienced by the young man, the patient, as he slowly unfolded these in the course of his treatment sessions; those experienced by the arts therapist, evoked by the situation, such as treating a man close to his own age or collaborating with a psychiatrist whose age, official standing, and mode of working (the medical model, anxiolytic drugs) differed from his own.

2. A head-teacher asks an arts therapist to assess and work with a five-year-old girl, whose hard-pressed class teacher has reported her as withdrawn and failing to progress in the reception group of 31 children. Very little is known about the child's family as they are 'not very forthcoming' and have not turned up at any parents' evenings. The head-teacher promises to notify the parents about the referral to the arts therapist who 'may wish to contact the parents directly'.

Here again the case is both a person and a situation. There are layers of predicaments: the child's; the head-teacher's, as she struggles to accommodate the needs of child and reception class teacher; and the arts therapist's, faced with approaching a 'not very forthcoming' family who have not yet been informed about her intervention. Who is going to become the 'case' in this instance? The five-year-old, or her family, or the school-staff, or the arts therapist?

3. One man (in his mid-fifties) stood out in the arts therapy group. He was more articulate than the other nine, he was the first to come and

last to leave. He was full of suggestions but as soon as one was taken up he would lose interest and his energies would go into drawing the group off on another tack. He usually supported anything the arts therapist said, sometimes to the point of embarrassment, but on one occasion he suddenly turned on the therapist and incited the rest of the group to riot.

The arts therapist (a man aged 26) chose this person as a subject for a case-study, partly because of the problems he posed in the group, partly because of the father-son associations that the patient's behaviour evoked in the arts therapist himself.

Roles and Relations

Questions

1. *What is your role vis-à-vis the patient and your colleagues?*

2. *What expectations and demands are you being loaded with?*

Any one of us, whatever our age, speaks with many voices: the voice of the Child from our past, or the voice of the (wise) Old Man or Woman from the future; the voice of impulse from the Id, or the voice of authoritarian constraint from the Super-ego; the voice of the Persona we want to show the world, or the voice of the Shadow we may try to disown. And so on.

If we assume that in any person, patient or professional, these many voices, or sub-personalities are jockeying for position, we can begin to see that in the most superficial exchanges of the case-study a large cast may be involved, though only two people may actually appear 'on stage' (see among others Moore 1990, Redfearn 1985). In the arts therapies, case-study is yet further enriched by the presence of a creative medium that may act as a lightning conductor for some of these sub-personalities.

Moreover, as we have seen, our case-study develops in the framework of a professional relation, an arrangement which itself is bound to increase the vocal polyphony and complexity.

Our role as professionals is shaped by a number of relations:

1. With a patient or group of patients.

2. With various other people in the system of which we are a part. These others may be associated with the patient through family or work-place; or they may be associated with us as fellow professionals, colleagues, friends, our own family.

To focus on our relation with patients. There will be times when our role will include elements from other types of two-person relations. It may on occasion closely approach that of various family members: parent (or grand-parent) and child; brother and sister; husband and wife. There will be times when the role may resemble that between teacher and pupil, or manager and managed. At yet other times, we may act the part of a good midwife, who facilitates the beneficial, natural processes of birth. A crucial element in any case-study rests on the professional's ability to spot these shifts in role.

A two-way relation that is asymmetric

The relation between patient and professional is two way; patients need professionals and, equally, professionals need patients. As professionals, we depend on patients using us, contributing experience and funds to the continuing growth of our knowledge and expertise. When we learn from the patient, we learn in the deepest sense: understanding ourselves as part and parcel of understanding the other.

One fundamental difference from friendship is that the relation between patient and professional is not evenly balanced or symmetric.

Particularly at the start of treatment, the patient is vulnerable, often dependent and highly suggestible. The degree of dependency varies. It tends to be higher in children, old people, the very ill, the psychotic. The degree of dependency goes closely though not co-terminously with the degree of trust. A central issue in therapy concerns the patient's continuing to trust the professional while growing independent. For many, as in infancy and childhood, a sense of trust can only grow with this increase in feeling and being independent. (After a long treatment, perhaps years after treatment has ended, it is not unknown for the asymmetry of patient and therapist to be reversed, with the patient now looking after the therapist who, in turn, is in a state of trust and dependence).

Asymmetry goes with responsibility and accountability

Asymmetry in the relation between patient and professional is reflected in such issues as responsibility and accountability, that is, the preparedness on the part of professionals to take charge of the situation and render an account of their actions to an appropriate other person. Here again degrees of responsibility and accountability may vary with degrees of vulnerability or dependency of the patient, with the status of the patient, or with the stage of treatment. In this context, a number of eventualities can sometimes cause prolonged heart-searching. Are all topics suitable for discussion in therapy since all relate to the patient's viewpoint, or are there some topics like politics or religion where the discussion should be closely guarded to avoid possible indoctrination? How far is the therapist responsible for a patient's suicidal attempt? And what should the therapist do when loaded with confidences that directly threaten someone else: sex abuse, intended rape or murder, a planned terrorist attack?

Moves to regulate the asymmetry

The issue of responsibility and accountability is tied up with the networks and hierarchies in which the case-study is conducted. Various moves have been designed to regulate the asymmetry of the relation between patient and professional.

1. PROFESSIONAL DISCIPLINES

On all professionals now are imposed disciplines with detailed training schemes, qualifications, and supervisory (watchdog) institutions. The debate on how best to balance what is on offer with what is demanded continues in the various societies and journals that have sprung up around these different professional disciplines. A growing body of research offers further opportunities for refining the appropriateness of fit between patient expectation and professional resource.

2. CONTRACTS

Certain ethical constraints, inherited in large part from the medical tradition reaching back to the Hippocratic oath, are built into the alliance between patient and professional. An unwritten understanding of rights on both sides, the rights of the patient and the rights of the professional, sometimes receives more formal expression in a contract, which might clarify, for example, the purpose of the case-study or the length of time it will last.

3. CONFIDENTIALITY

Various sanctions underpin the alliance including the important one of confidentiality, that bedrock on which the mutual trust between patient and professional is founded.

These contracts and sanctions bear on the role of professional as researcher just as much as they bear on the day to day 'clinical' exchanges. They may extend into and clash with other contractual arrangements, written or unwritten, in other areas of the patient's or the professional's life, such as the family or the work-place. Many parents, for example, find it hard to discover that they do not always share confidences their child has revealed to the professional. Controversies sometimes arise over whether outsiders, such as police or insurance companies, should have access to a patient's confidential record.

A specific feature for arts therapists: The role of the arts-medium

These are some of the more general issues arising in connection with our role as professionals. Arts therapists face a further question. Sometimes this takes the following form: Are we psychotherapists using a creative mode of intervention or are we artists using a psychotherapeutic mode to practise our art? (see Feder and Feder 1981). As the force of imagination finds increasing recognition in the theory and practice of psychotherapy, this apparent dilemma may loom less prominently. But what will not go away is the fact that, in any arts therapy, a third member further complicates an already complex situation. This 'tertium datum', is the arts medium itself which often serves as a vehicle for the exchanges between patient and therapist and as expression of the growing relation between them.

The role of the medium assumes an especially obvious and solid form in art therapy where many features of the exchange between the pair are openly transferred to the art-object, a painting or a sculpture. But this transfer also occurs in therapies where the medium is not as concrete as a picture. Exchanges of roles and relations may be transferred into a sequence of music, movement, or drama. Indeed, such a transfer is a crucial source of strength for all the arts therapies.

A Practical Exercise in Exploring Roles

In coming to grips with our complex role, you may find the following exercise of some value in distinguishing the levels in the complexity. First, think of anyone you know and describe this other person as though you were standing at a window looking out on to him or her from a position of detachment.

When you have finished that description, bring yourself into the scene outside the window, and now record what goes on when you and this other person are working and playing together as Us.

When you have finished that, develop your two descriptions into an imaginative 'walk' using the arts medium of your choice: an 'automatic' improvisation with colours and lines, sounds and songs, movements and dance, or a piece of theatre.

The three levels in this exercise represent the three aspects of our role, the three foci of growth in understanding the other and ourselves. In presenting any case, we are caught up in an incompatibility. On the one hand, we settle into a description where we find ourselves detached, separate from, albeit interested in, an other. On the other hand, as we become involved in the act and content of the description, we find ourselves slipping into the position of the person we are studying, the better to reach what we are seeking to describe. We may alight on feelings in ourselves evoked not just by the effort of description, but stemming directly from this other, who may well be successfully eluding us as long as we continue the search to understand. The case-study, along with any art-medium, provides a space for bridging these incompatible complementarities. The understanding that arises from our interactions with another person and the medium (the sense of Us) feeds into our understanding of that Other (the detached Him or Her), and in cyclical fashion feeds into and stabilizes these interactions. We become a central part of any growth in understanding the Other. As in physics, there is no such thing as a detached observer who is not influencing the experiment.

Two further developments follow from this exercise:

1. Learning about (by reading books, or taking instructions), as distinct from learning through involvement in an emotional experience.

2. Being there (in empathy and reverie), so that the other learns without interpretations or instructions which implicitly undermine the sense of being his or her own person.

Orientation

Questions

1. What is your place in the system (of healing, education, etc)?

2. Who are your colleagues?

3. What is your patient's place in this system?

A description of the networks and hierarchies in the system in which a case-study is conducted, starting out from the patient or group, would include:

1. Relatives. Especially relevant when the patient is a child (family therapy) or a heavily dependent person (a psychotic patient or one suffering from Alzheimer's disease or senility or severe physical or mental handicap).

2. People from the patient's work-place. Teachers and hierarchies within the school. The hierarchy of work-mates (managers and personnel officers).

3. Social workers, probation officers, and hierarchies in their respective services.

4. Referring agents, especially doctors and the NHS or private practice networks.

5. Therapist's colleagues. Other arts therapists and their networks. Other therapists (physio-, occupational, speech and language, psycho- etc). Psychologists (educational, industrial, clinical). Psychiatrists. (For further definitions of these specialities see dictionaries such as Rycroft 1968, and Stuart-Hamilton 1994 a, b, and c).

6. Treatment institutions, doctors and associated staff, and the hierarchy in hospitals. Here ambiguities may arise since the senior staff are often the least permanent members and have the least day to day contact with patients (see Higgins 1963(a)).

The Case as a Unique Instance or an Example of a Generality

The case-study is the bedrock of social or clinical work. Every fledgling social science or medical student, at the start of practical studies, is introduced to the idea of a case and to 'taking the history' of a case. A *vade mecum* for the medical student on clinical methods opens with the categorical statement: 'There can be no questioning the value of accurate and systematic case-taking. It trains the beginner in habits of thoroughness and exactness at the bedside and ensures that no point of importance in a case is missed'. For the experienced clinician, systematic case-taking offers to his experience a 'concrete embodiment' for future comparisons and future knowledge (Hutchison and Hunter 1945).

The question behind these statements is: what is the case-study for? What is the purpose of the history-taking? The authors of *Clinical Methods* address the medical model where the nature of any case (the demand) tends to be defined as a breakdown in physical systems, the body and its environment. The type of breakdown becomes classified into a system of diseases and of environmental agents which bring about these diseases. Similarly, the type of remedy becomes classified into a system which interlocks with this system of disease. The practice of medicine becomes an exercise in labelling a patient as well or ill, and if ill, defining the specific illness, for example cancer, hypercholesterolaemia, neurosis, depression, psychosis, or emotional and behavioural disorder (EBD). In the medical model, core concepts are illness, cause, and cure. The primary task lies in diagnosing the disease, and slotting it in with the appropriate remedy. In the medical model, the primary task in a case-study is to delineate this process of diagnosis and remedy.

In psychological and arts therapies, a somewhat different primary task determines a somewhat different case-study. Here the expertise lies in understanding different levels of mental functioning: the so-called unconscious processes and the symbolism associated with these. The field, as in medicine, involves human biology but the resource on offer is the mapping out of meaning (often through the use of a powerful medium such as rhythm, colour, line, body movement, narrative), and the establishment in the patient of a sense of being understood, of someone getting the meaning right. The primary task of the case-study is the record of this understanding (see further Rycroft 1985, Zinkin 1987, Aldridge 1990 and 1991, Hansen 1991, Seedhouse 1991, Reason *et al.* 1992, Mitchell Noon 1992).

The dual reference to person and situation in the word 'case' opens up a major distinction in case-studies: namely, whether the person is presented as an example of a situation or as a unique entity existing in his or her own right. This distinction will inevitably influence the nature and direction of arts therapy case-studies let alone any research based on them.

The case as example forms the basis of medicine and law. Doctors repeatedly speak of the latest case of 'flu or depression, or of that case which responded so well (or badly) to the latest treatment. A slow shift, however, has occurred in case-studies when patients begin to stand out from the descriptive pages not as examples, cyphers, or symbols, but as persons unique in their own right, inimitable and unreplicable.

This shift becomes apparent in the early works of Freud, who ostensibly used case-histories as the hooks on which to hang his theories of psychological mechanisms: Dora was presented to illustrate the patterns of hysteria; Little Hans to illustrate a childhood phobia; the Rat Man and the Wolf Man to illustrate obsessional states; Dr Schreber to illustrate the paranoid psychosis which often lies at the back of these obsessional states.

Yet as we read these case-studies we become aware that Dora, Little Hans and the rest are stepping out of their role as examples. His dealings with Dora forced Freud to recognise the transference. The subject who had started as an example of one situation (hysteria), by dint of her role in the drama changed into an example of quite a different situation, one in which the writer was every bit as involved as she was. Dora in Freud's writing comes through as a person in her own right, a microcosm, and case-study as a means of connecting science and art. The issue of the unique characterises imaginative writing in plays and novels.

With a firm base in an imaginative medium, arts therapists are well placed to take advantage of the changing emphasis on the unique (see further in Chapter IX).

Essential Patterns in a Case-Study

To undertake a case-study is to have a foot in both science and art. Indeed it is to experience the fallacy of any rigid distinction between these two domains. Some of these deeper issues in case-study are examined in greater detail in the last two chapters of this book. Here it is only necessary to remind ourselves that case-study bears a close affinity to biography and biography as an aspect of history has always been seen as operating on the bridge between science and art (see Shelston 1977).

In intermediate sections of the book, we will look at different areas relevant in any case-study: how and why a person comes to a therapist (referral); what actually brings him or her (complaints); family background; personal past; transformations in that amalgam of nature and nurture we know as personality.

As any case-study grows, these areas, which may start out in the student's mind as discrete 'boxes' of information, will often be found to sprout connections and coalesce. The problems a patient presents may slowly come to be seen as a natural evolution, an inevitable consequence of family and personal background, these two facets of the background being increasingly hard to disentangle. In this evolution, the positive forces in a joint family and personal background come to exert a prominent influence on how patients resolve their problems.

A good case-study, like a good story or good piece of music, starts with the germ of an idea, a bizarre complaint, for example, such as the man who mistook his wife for a hat (Sacks 1986) and slowly unfolds into a diagnosis. Such an unfolding yields abundant opportunities for the archaeological sleuth to make sense of the past or for the science fiction addict to watch for the confirmation of his predictions.

CHAPTER II

The Referral

Some questions to be considered before the patient is seen, i.e., search based on available information in notes, staff discussions, and so on.

1. *Do you have the patient's permission to be involved in the case, and in the confidential information being passed to you?*

2. *What is the route the referral has taken to reach you?*

3. *What are the nature of the difficulties as defined by the different people involved in the referral: the patient, relatives, friends, his/her colleagues, your colleagues, staff and others?*

4. *How are the difficulties affecting the life of the patient and those about him/her?*

5. *How has the patient coped with life in the past? What aspects of his/her life did he/she enjoy or find satisfying? What has he/she achieved? What does he/she appear to feel proud of?*

6. *What are the expectations about treatment?*

7. *What previous treatments, particularly psychiatric and arts therapy treatment, have been tried?*

8. *What are some of the outstanding past experiences?*

9. *What sort of childhood experiences did he/she appear to have?*

10. *Who made up his/her family or substitute family? Who were the key figures?*

11. *What about schooling and later education?*

12. *What about jobs, satisfaction and difficulties in work? Plans and ambitions?*

13. *What about leisure activities, hobbies, holidays? Secret ambitions dating from childhood?*

14. *Is the patient single, engaged, married, separated, divorced, widowed? The nature of intimate relations, enjoyments, unhappiness, and phantasies?*

15. *What are the present domestic circumstances? Financial burdens and anxieties?*

16. *How does the patient relate to his/her body? Is there awareness, concern, denial? Any past experiences or present interests in movement, music, painting, poetry, plays or stories?*

17. *What sort of a person comes through from descriptions in the notes? Do you expect to see this person or someone quite different?*

Being Forewarned: Advantages and Disadvantages

As a general principle, reconnaissance makes sense. Sifting issues before we become entrenched in them, spying out the land, assessing future risks, considering possible strategies, pegging out expectations, all these must strike us as prudent moves. There is no doubt that we can learn a lot about some patients before actually meeting them. From the same sources, we can also learn much about the people we are going to be working with, the network we are going to have to slot into. Our reconnaissance before meeting patients often includes the social and institutional context in which they pass their lives.

Valuable though such reconnaissance may be, it has also to be said that all such initial pre-meeting explorations should be made with the greatest tact and circumspection. For as in foetal life, the earlier the event, the more momentous its potential consequences; although there is no doubt that we can learn much about possible future developments, there is also no doubt that we can seriously prejudice these by a false move.

The first of such hazards is implicit in the phrase already used of 'spying out the land'. Even though a patient gives open consent to our exploration (and the exploration should never be embarked on without adequate assurances that such consent has been given – not always as easy an exercise as it might seem) the apparent openness is likely to be hedged about with many overt and many more unconscious reservations. (Who is this person intruding on our lives? Upsetting the status quo? Digging up our secrets? Dr A. didn't really want to bring her in. You could see it in his face when he said he'd write the letter). Patients are as quick to pick up unconscious feelings of inter-professional rivalry as children to pick up unconscious antagonisms between their parents.

Students embarking on this pre-meeting reconnaissance will find themselves immediately impaled on the horns of an all-too-familiar dilemma: if we make no preliminary exploration, we are jettisoning valuable safeguards and could be accused of lack of interest; if we do explore, albeit with consent, we may be accused of intruding.

The first disadvantage, then, about pre-meeting reconnaissance is that in undertaking it, we can easily be nudged into the role of a spy or at any rate of someone who has listened at length to the prosecution (perhaps even sided with it) before hearing the defendant.

The second disadvantage distills the reality out of the first: any written or verbal record with which we are plied is cast in the language of the writer or speaker and therefore is bound to carry, however minimally, the writer's or speaker's prejudices. In imbibing these we can in no way claim to be immune to their effects. Bion advocated that before any session the therapist should seek to rid his mind of all memories and desires, these harbingers of therapists' prejudices which, if unharnessed, could jeopardise their work (Bion 1977). The same principle, on a larger canvas, goes for the recording of a case-study; we might certainly advance the argument that before seeing patients we should minimise our exposure to other people's prejudices about them.

The Referral Letter and Other Sources of Pre-Meeting Knowledge

Among the sources for our pre-meeting knowledge, perhaps the commonest is the referral note or letter inviting us to become involved with the case. The writer may be the patient (or in the case of a child, one or both parents) or the patient's doctor (family practitioner or consultant) or a non-medical person such as a teacher, social worker, counsellor, or member of the clergy or police.

From this referral letter we can often establish some important facts:

1. The relation of the referrer to the patient. How long have the two known each other? How have they got on together?

2. Is the referral letter written with the patient's full consent? Does the patient know the gist of its content as well as the fact of its being sent? Does it convey implied or explicit secrets about the patient? Does the patient know about these revelations?

3. Are other people besides the patient implicated in the letter? A spouse, for example, or other family members. Do these others know about the letter?

4. What is the nature of the problem as defined by the referrer? How far would the patient be expected to agree with this definition? Put differently, were we to ask the patient subsequently why he or she had come to see us, would we expect to hear an account similar to the one we read in the letter, or something quite different? For example, a consultant physician asks an art therapist to see a twelve-year-old girl in his ward because she is 'refusing to co-operate in the treatment'. When seen the girl says she is scared stiff of the treatment, wants to do what she's told but can't understand what the consultant says. He uses long words that confuse her.

5. How deeply have others already involved you in the referral? What expectations have been set up for the patient and others about your involvement? Has the patient been told you will see him or her? Or simply that you have been consulted about the possibility of doing so? How far has your autonomy, your capacity to make your own decisions, been respected?

6. To what extent is the act of referral registering an unloading of anxiety on the part of the referrer? Any referral is by its nature a request for assistance with all the ambiguities which go with such a request. A key element in the subsequent development of any case rests on whether and how these ambiguities are explored, exposed, and resolved.

7. What sort of a person is writing this referral note and what sort of a relationship can you expect to develop with the writer in your subsequent work with the patient?

Another source of data is the extant case record. If this is a medical file, it may vary from the family practitioner one-liners (a single card covering decades) to the fat hospital document which achieved its girth in the course of one short stay. Or the case record at the student's disposal may be an educational file with test-results, reports, and the various assessments that now play a prominent part in a child's school career. These assessments are devised by combined teams of teachers, educational psychologists, speech therapists and others. They are often required by government policies. Their explicit objective is to monitor progress and to detect early signs of difficulty so that appropriate steps may be taken to meet any special need.

A third source of pre-meeting knowledge comes from free-floating unwritten discussion with those already involved with the patient.

The Sharing of Anxieties

When a patient is referred to someone else, it is an open acknowledgement that the referrer cannot cope with the situation on his or her own. He may be too busy. He may want to involve an extra pair of hands like a builder who at times needs an assistant. He may feel the case involves areas of expertise which lie outside his sphere of competence. Or there may be something about the case which triggers off a load of anxiety which he or she cannot contain.

Medicine with its clear division of specialities and consultant teams encourages a respect for expertise. Seemingly with good reason. For, after all, who would want to have a kidney removed by a dermatologist? But there are snags. A well-recognised problem in medicine is the patient who shops around, the so-called chronic somatiser, who collects consultations with specialist departments, often without these departments having any inkling of what is going on. The wider the range of departments available for choice (the domain of shopping around) the more extensive the multiple consultation network (see Bass and Murphy 1990).

When it comes to matters of the mind, the boundaries of expertise become less clear-cut. How far is the professional (whether psychiatrist, psychologist, or psychotherapist) an expert in the running of someone else's school-class, let alone someone else's family or person. Indeed a central plank in the professional's expertise is often defined as assisting a person to be his or her own man or woman. How far can the professional exercise this expertise when invited to trespass and take over this very territory of personal decisions?

The resolution of this paradox frequently turns on how people's anxieties are actually being dealt with in a referral. Once the unloading of anxiety is recognised, the issue is no longer the stark one of whether or not a referral is accepted, whether, that is, the person to whom the case is referred simply takes over or refuses to take over the referrer's anxieties. Instead there is the possibility of some debate, some sharing of anxieties: two heads, an extra pair of hands.

The Interview

Some basic questions about the interview

1. *What is the context in which the interview is taking place? Is it a one-off meeting? Or the start of a series?*

2. *Linked with your answer to question 1, what is your main objective in the interview? To gather information in order to lay out a plan of*

action? To establish a longer-term relation with the patient in which some change may be expected?

3. *In the light of 1 and 2, what balance are you striking in the interview between participating and observing?*

4. *How are you distinguishing objective and subjective worlds?*

5. *How are you verifying facts and inferences in these objective and subjective worlds?*

6. *What is the balance in your data between verbatim and remembered report? What further analysis are you conducting on your verbatim reports or videos or patients' creative products?*

7. *What are the transference and counter-transference data in your case-study?*

8. *What significant events did not happen or have not been mentioned?*

The interview serves a number of purposes. First, it offers an occasion to forge some sort of relationship. There are many subtle nuances in how this happens (for some timely sidelights on medical interviews see Bodley Scott 1965). Second, it provides a standard neutral situation against which to assess patients' behaviour, including what they say, how they say it, and the many paralinguistic gestures such as facial expression, tone of voice, associated movements. Third, it offers an opportunity for gathering information at first-hand, without its being sifted through another's viewpoint.

These three purposes are subtly inter-related. The more the patient trusts the interviewer, the more information is likely to be divulged. The information is likely to be more reliable since there is less need for defences to suppress or distort it.

At any interview a two-way communication is struck at a number of levels:

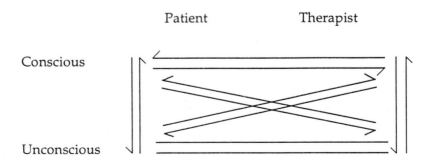

This pattern of communications, the constant feedback (or lack of it) between patient and interviewer, determines how an interview flows (or gets stuck). Tapping this interactive flow (the so-called transference and counter-transference awareness of the interviewer) often provides the most accurate record of what is going on.

One of the hardest tasks in an interview is to control the depth of the patient's trust, which may develop from the very first moment of the meeting or before. In theory, this depth of trust should be tailored in accordance with the number of encounters predicted. If only one or two interviews are planned, then a degree of detachment on the part of the interviewer would be appropriate in order to limit the patient's trust and expectation, and to spare him or her unnecessary suffering. In practice, this is easier said than done. Under these conditions, the interviewer is often caught between two conflicting pulls: the search for information; and a detached stance designed to limit the flow.

Interviewers are observers and at the same time they are participants in the events being observed. The distinction overlaps the one made by Martin Buber between the I-Thou and the I-It. In the confrontation I-Thou, we commingle with another person on an equal footing; in the confrontation I-It, we assume a detached observer, 'scientific' stance towards this other person or object (Buber 1952). Buber's distinction harks back to our earliest human experiences. I-Thou predates I-It; I-It clarifies I-Thou. We resort to I-It when I-Thou becomes overwhelming; I-Thou generates the initial sparks for learning. An internal I-Thou occurs in our free associations when we reach out for the meaning of dream images or other 'unconscious' experiences. I-Thou is the basis of transference and counter-transference intuitions. We still need I-It to articulate these. The arts provide a space in which this subjective I-Thou is externalised.

Data and Relations

The balance interviewers strike between being an observer and being a participant depends in part on how deeply they can afford to be involved in any particular case. This degree of involvement, this balance between observer and participant, is one way in which relations influence the data that are collected in a case-study.

The degree of involvement is an example of a more general principle: the context in which we take soundings can influence profoundly the soundings we take. We all present different aspects of ourselves in different circumstances or under different conditions. We speak more freely when we trust the person we are talking to; we tailor (consciously and unconsciously) our behaviour and what we say to people, according to the image we have of them and according to what we think they want to hear. We may wish to please or placate them or conversely we may aim to test or thwart them.

These shifts in what we say according to the context in which we say it are often very apparent in children, who may clam up as soon as a parent joins the interview or, conversely, who may suddenly find their voice when this happens. In a condition of childhood known as elective mutism, the child maps out networks of those who can be communicated with and those who can't. Among those who can be communicated with, there is a further mapping of what messages are broadcast and what not.

Elective mutism is an exaggerated form of what happens to us all and should serve as a reminder of how important it is in a case-study to be aware of the context in which information is imparted.

Fact, Inference, and Verification

Subjective and objective worlds

In a case-study, we are engaged in two related enquiries. The first has to do with building up a picture of the world as the patient sees it, his or her subjective world. In the second type of enquiry, we aim to build up a picture of the patient's life as others see it. Somewhere in this second view, beyond the distortions which we and others can clearly introduce as a result of our own subjective worlds, we hope to reach a more balanced assessment of events in which the patient was involved. We aspire to a detached and unbiased measure, an objective world against which the subjective worlds can be compared.

Examples of objective fact might be a patient's name, date of birth, or address. If given falsely, the error can be checked and corrected according to a key scientific principle of falsifiability. Yet when it comes to case-study none of these objective facts turn out to be as cut-and dried as they might appear.

Consider for a moment the seemingly straightforward fact of a person's age. A patient states with conviction that she is twenty-four. Her mother insists that she is thirty-four and produces a copy of the birth-certificate to prove this. Our dual enquiry in a case-study requires that we consider, as far as is appropriate:

1. The nature of the patient's conviction. Is she genuinely convinced, that is, deluded, about her age? Is she aware that she is telling a not-so-unusual white lie?

2. The reason for her maintaining that she is ten years younger than she is.

3. The role of the mother as a reality-fixer.

Any one of these three considerations, which have to do with a subjective world, may prove as significant in the case-study as establishing the patient's age in an objective world.

These two parallel and often complementary directions of enquiry stem from what earlier I called the asymmetry in the therapist's role. On the one hand, we are called upon to be the person who understands, empathises with, the patient; to do this properly we have to try to see the world through his or her eyes. On the other hand, we are called upon to assist in moves to expand this personal world which has become in the patient's own eyes restrictive and crippling. To do this properly we need to take objective soundings through which we can point to the limitations, the phantasy distortions, which are bringing about these restrictions.

Though in theory the distinction between subjective and objective worlds holds, in practice it becomes less clear when we realise how much we use the subjective to interpret the objective. There is an ever-changing circle which relates what we perceive to our memories, our values, and our psychological 'set'. We learn about an Other by empathising with him/her, but we arrive at this empathic understanding in large part by our subjective experience. The relation between subjective and objective worlds is like that between opposite sides of the same coin (see further in Mason 1990).

Verification

The laws of evidence apply in both types of enquiry, whether into subjective or objective worlds. In both we need to distinguish between an empirical fact and a logical inference, and to relate the two through a system of verification (see Hospers 1967).

A patient says he sees a stick with a knob on the end of it protruding from a wall. We look at the place on the wall he is pointing to and see only the handle on the door of a cupboard. The fact in the patient's world is what he says he sees, though of course there may be all sorts of complications at the back of this fact (he may be lying, i.e., know he is presenting a false fact). The fact in the objective world is the discrepancy between what he says he sees and what any other observer sees, that is, that he is labouring under an illusion.

Hallucinations, illusions, delusions, like dreams, emotional states, and bodily feelings, are statements about a personal world; subjective facts which in one sense we can never verify objectively. All we can do where perceptions and memories are concerned is to check whether a subjective report is corroborated by someone else. If a patient sees a rat running across the floor and the therapist sees it too, then (unless there is folie à deux) an objective fact confirms subjective observations. If the therapist does not see the rat, this may be because the therapist was not looking in the right direction at the time: a subjective observation has yet to be verified as an objective fact. Or it may be because the patient is seeing something which is not there (i.e., hallucinating) or pretending to see it when he does not (i.e., lying).

To return to our patient with the knob on the wall. If, while speaking about it, he runs his hands across a bulge on the front of his trousers, we may infer that the image he sees on the wall is standing for (symbolising) his awareness of an erection. If he refers to a phallus while describing the knob, or draws it or enlarges on a story of sexual exploits, our inference about some facts in his subjective world is verified.

We are confronted constantly with facts (subjective and objective), and we make inferences which we then need to verify or turn into facts. Concerning our patient, our inference may be quite misguided. The bulge on the front of his trousers may turn out to be an apple, which he is fingering with a view to eating as soon as the interview is over. The illusion he built on the door handle may have symbolised a branch of an apple-tree, or a magic staff which offers him escape as soon as he is free to leave the room.

As different human types with different styles, we have our individual ways of verifying our inferences. If we rely heavily on thinking, or if we are obsessional, we may methodically distinguish the facts we have established from the hypotheses we have proposed. If we rely predominantly on our intuitions, or have over the years built up a fund of experience, we are more likely to risk by-passing the painstaking pedestrian effort of distinguishing fact from inference. The speed at which we move and our capacity for patience may also enter the equation.

Verbatim and Remembered Report

The sources on which students rely for building a case-study include their own and others' written reports, patients' creative products, hearsay evidence from staff discussions, their own and others' test results, tape or video-recordings.

In any record written at the time or subsequently, there are a number of biases. For a start, in the written record, we can never adequately convey the intrinsic difference between written and spoken word (see Henry Green's essay 'A novelist to his readers' in Green 1992). Then we have to allow for the bias of the human recorder. We select from what we see and remember and slant our record in the light of what determines this selectivity.

In an effort to minimise this bias, the student may seek to write down verbatim what a patient says or use a tape- or video-recorder for the same purpose. Apart from the accuracy of such reports, one great advantage (especially of mechanical recorders) is that an interview, or sections of it, can be re-played as often as required. Other observers' responses to an identical record can be obtained. The record can be rated and compared with others.

The obvious snag about attempting to clutch a verbatim record is the effect the various moves employed must have on the context in which the data are being collected, and so on the data themselves. Patients, not only the paranoidally inclined, respond differently to an interviewer who is preoccupied with getting their exact words into a note-book, or constantly glancing at the clicking and whirring of a mechanical recorder, than they do to a quiet listener giving whole-hearted attention to understanding the meaning of their words at all different levels. Mechanical contrivances which are introduced in the service of research or objectivity, do unfortunately often represent an intrusion into an intimacy which lies at the heart of a good case-study. This intrusion affects both therapist and patient, sometimes at the most sensitive points of interaction.

Anthropologists (see Mayer 1989) have noted a not dissimilar result when, after the most elaborate field recordings and note-taking, the one experience which recaptures a scene and brings new insights is a memory stirred years later and in a completely different setting by an unexpected and seemingly irrelevant event such as the smell of burning leaves or the taste of the madeleine cake in Proust's *A la Recherche du Temps Perdu*.

Contributions from the arts media

Different arts products fall somewhere between a verbatim and remembered record. Like a sound or video tape, they are concrete objects which can serve as repeated reminders of an occasion and which others besides patient and therapist can examine and comment on (with the patient's permission). Examples: for the student art therapist, a painting or drawing by the patient may vividly represent family members as seen in the present or past; for the student of dance/movement therapy, a video of modes of moving may reveal essential personal characteristics that cry out for development. The patients' expressions in creative media are especially valuable when it comes to assessing intellect, thought processes, orientation, emotions, the harmony of body and mind.

The nature of the medium by means of which we communicate can influence the communication itself. We observe this most directly when interpretations, our own or those of our patients, are loaded with a poetic quality in wording or idea. The point is taken up further in the final chapter of the book.

Transference and Counter-Transference

Arguably the most important source of information comes from our analysis of the impact the patient has on us, as therapists, and vice versa, the impact we have on the patient.

This impact can take many forms: our feelings (love, hate, anger, guilt, shame), the role we see ourselves cast in at any time (good parent, bad parent, good child, bad child, grandparent, friend, piece of furniture), how we are being cast in it (gratefully, gently, pressurised, incised, stuffed) and how this role relates to experiences from our own present and past history. It is important to recognise these forms of impact though not necessarily to write them down. Indeed, they are sometimes shifting so fast that it would be impossible to keep track of them in a note-book.

This impact is not confined to the times we are with the patient. It can crop up at any time, make itself felt in our dreams or when we are ostensibly doing something quite different. Remembered in tranquillity, the impact can provoke associations that can often shed the clearest light on what is happening between us and our patients and so in the patients themselves.

This impact of the patient on us is known as counter-transference. Transference is the impact we have on patients, the feelings we arouse in them and which they may attribute to us, the roles they cast us in, and the relations these roles bear to figures from their personal subjective world, past and present.

Early on in his taking down of case-histories, Freud found that he was recording not a true account of historical events but phantasies of events as if they had actually happened. The material of a case-history is fictive in that it includes descriptions of dreams, passions, wishes, symptoms, which cannot be witnessed by anyone else, and, moreover, are inevitably distorted in the telling by the psychological bias of the teller (hysterical splits, paranoid slants, depressive or elated moods etc). The therapist is quickly swept into this fiction in which to the historical record is now added the record of transference and counter-transference, since the therapist is no more immune to the fictive nature of his own material than is the patient. Like all good fiction, indeed all imaginative work, structures are available for steering a course through the maelstrom. These structures include story, plot, narrative, and the patterns which underlie them. To these we will return in Chapter IX.

Un-History

One final point about the information we collect is the significance of what is *not* collected. I mean by this not just silent communications, and not just information that is held back purposely or in unawareness. But I mean that in any situation behind events that happen, and sentences that are uttered, there is another world of events that didn't happen and sentences that weren't voiced. This is the world of un-history and one we often play with. 'What would have happened if A had met B before marrying C?' 'Suppose she'd never taken that job?'

Memory, on which we rely so heavily in collecting a case-history, has to be read as separate from history. It is not a reliable guide to history since in remembering we omit and falsify. Through memory, we make a different history from the one that happened. When we remember we often confabulate and in this sense we connect with un-history, with pre-historical images, and with events that have not yet happened.

The value of reflecting on this world of un-history is the clues it can offer about the inevitability of what did happen, or what would have happened in the end even if a different direction had been taken. For what remains unsaid in us may on the one hand be waiting to come into view, or on the other hand become available for someone else to express if we don't.

So being aware of this world which did not emerge but which is always around can bring relief in two further ways. It can take some of the pressure off our desire to make the unconscious conscious, to keep constant checks on our dreams or our counter-transference. If we know that whatever emerges must always have a shadow un-emergence, we can trust the unconscious to evolve at its own pace; we need not be for ever peering into its evolution and chivvying it. Unconscious forces find their way into history through the meshes of un-history. Patients may harbour their own salvation more often than those caring for them may be able to admit.

Furthermore, from this awareness of un-history, and our consequent trusting of unconscious evolution, we may be less anxious over missing an event that has emerged, failing to interpret a particular message from the unconscious at a particular time, or getting this interpretation wrong. In the slow integration of the inevitable, of history and un-history, these mistakes will be ironed out. They may even emerge as necessary stimulants for change.

This is not to advocate the making of mistakes (patients can certainly die as a result of ignorance, negligence, or misreadings on the part of those looking after them) but to suggest that we adopt a less omnipotent and guilt-laden attitude to mistakes when they occur (patients can also transcend as a result of the same defective interventions).

CHAPTER III

The Complaint

Questions for eliciting complaints from the patient and others

1. *What in your patient's own words is the main complaint? What other complaints are voiced by the patient?*

2. *With regard to each of these complaints, how long have they been going on? When did the patient first notice the change? What was happening in the patient's life at the time? Is any particular event associated with the start or development of these complaints? (e.g. changes in the family such as the advent of a brother or sister? Or changes in love-life? Or in work? Or in social life?)*

3. *Has the illness been associated with changes in biological rhythms? Sleep, eating, drinking, excreting, sexual drive? Changes in body shape (weight and height) or appearance (loss of hair, colouring)?*

4. *Has the illness gone with changes in the patient's response to those around? Is it easier or harder to talk to people, make decisions, assume responsibility?*

5. *What was patient's response to the illness when it started? And subsequently?*

6. *What information does the patient impart about him or her self? How is it imparted? In words? Or in non-verbal expressions?*

7. *What are others complaining about the patient? About themselves? About related topics?*

8. *What is not being said by these various voices of complaint? Is some general topic notable by its absence? (e.g. no complaints against oneself in the melee of complaints against others, or no reference to the psyche in complaints about the body). Or are the gaps across the voices? (e.g. the symmetry of such absences in a conjugal dispute).*

9. *How seriously are the complaints taken at conscious or unconscious levels? By the complainer or by others? How much does a complaint*

*imply that something must be done about it? How far are we drawn
to James Thurber's response to the letter sent him saying 'we have
mice on our mantelpiece': Is this a boast or do you want some
action?*

10. *Can you see a pattern in the various sets of complaints?*

11. *Do the complaints change over time? How?*

12. *Does the mode of complaining change over time? How?*

Viewpoints in Complaints

Complaints come in any form and number. There is the single complaint
that pins down complainer and those around:

> 'This tooth-ache... I've had it all the week-end and I can't think of
> anything else'.

> 'When I get this migraine the only thing to do is to go to bed in a
> dark room and wait till it's over'.

> 'Nag... nag... nag. She never lets up. I tell you it's driving us crazy'.

> 'He's obsessed with this jealousy. Everything comes back to it. He
> wraps me up in it so that I become as trapped as he is. Our life's
> become *intolerable*'.

> 'I can't get the accident out of my mind. Every night I dream about
> it. I'm in the ship again. It's dark and the water's rising. And the
> only thing I can hear are the screams'.

Or there is a whole string of complaints, sometimes fragmented and
dis-connected, sometimes grouped into what has become a recognised
syndrome (for further details see Chapter VII).

> 'And another thing I get are these pains in the side of my head. They
> shoot all over and go down the neck and join up with the ones I told
> you about that come up from my right wrist. Then there's the rash
> that comes out on my shins and stays and stays until the summer.
> (I never seem to get it in the summer.) Sometimes I get another sort
> of rash under my arms. Heat-rash a doctor once called it but it's
> often worse in the middle of the winter. Oh yes and I get diarrhoea
> if I eat more than two apples a day. I used to get dreadful
> pre-menstrual cramps but they're a bit better now that I've had the
> menopause. The worst thing at the moment are these fluttery
> vibrations in the back passage like as though there's about to be an
> explosion and the whole of my insides fall out. What else is there?

I've made a list here to be sure I didn't leave anything out'. (See also Beckitt 1959)

'He's always on the go. In and out of everything. Can't settle to any game for more than five minutes. Keeps on at me: what can I do now, mum? tell me what can I do now? Any room he's been playing in it's like a hurricane's hit it. He infuriates the daylights out of his dad who's an orderly man. His father's always shouting at him: You live in a permanent shambles. He's wrecking our household with his carry-on. At school, it's just the same. Can't sit still long enough to learn his letters and his exercise books, when he can find them, are atrocious'.

'When she was an infant she had these rashes. Then she became chesty and wheezy and they said she had asthma and now she gets dreadful hay fever and is sick every time my husband paints the house'.

There is the complaint that upsets the patient so that he or she obviously wants to do something about it, and complaints that mainly upset those around and leave the patient relatively undisturbed. There is the complaint that means what it says; and the complaint which means something quite different. There's the complaint that ought to be there but isn't; and the complaint that ought not to be there but is.

Complaints and symptoms are a way of entering history, both a personal history and history on a larger scale. Like some illnesses, complaints may be subject to waves of fashion. The symptoms of conversion hysteria, for example, are much less frequently seen now than they were in the days of Charcot.

The following discrepancies should be borne in mind:

1. The complaints that are voiced by patients are not necessarily the complaints which are really troubling them.

2. Patients may know about this discrepancy between voiced and withheld complaint (cf. the issues of embarrassment, purposeful obfuscation), or they may not (cf. issues of awareness and insight, see David 1990).

3. Complaints voiced or withheld do not necessarily refer accurately to undercurrent experiences, such as wishes, fears, expectations, intentions.

4. The complaints voiced by others may bear little relation to the complaints experienced by the patient.

5. The reasons for referral, as stated in referral letters and so forth, may turn out to be different from the real reasons for referral, either at the time or subsequently.

6. These real reasons for referral, either as stated or as implied, may differ from the complaints or undercurrent experiences of the patient or others at the time or subsequently.

The Occurrence of Illness

A number of points are worth bearing in mind about illness in general. The first is that illnesses of all descriptions occur in the context of our life-path and the more we know about this life-path the more we can appreciate the meaning or significance of any illness for the sufferer. Illnesses are rarely random or 'accidental' events.

The meaning lies both in the point of time when we become ill and in the nature of the illness itself. People often fall ill at turning-points in their lives: young men and women when setting out on a career the choice of which turns out to have been inappropriate; older men and women when they retire. At these turning-points, we are often particularly concerned with disentangling the true from the false selves which we may have worn for years. We may have put on these false selves in the first place because we were trapped in no-win situations. A young woman becomes schizophrenic as she attempts to sort out her involvement in a family lie. She has spent her life trying to please her father. But whatever she does is wrong. Her most generous actions simply sour the situation. She goes mad and as a result explodes the family 'secret' that he is not in fact her father at all but a man who hated her because her mother cuckolded him after he had an accident. Or a child becomes 'frantic and quite out of hand' because he senses he is not being told the truth about his mother's death and won't let anyone rest until he is.

The second point about illness is that its onset often reveals an imbalance in the lifestyle. Besides exploding lies we have lived with, false selves and inadequate solutions we have adopted in our attempts to cope, an illness can point to physical or mental resources which we are abusing or not using. The outcome of an illness may result in a new configuration, a new setting for balance and imbalance. In this sense, illness provides an example of what Jung meant by the emergence of the shadow. Illness is to health what the shadow is to the substance. The shadow shows up the missing features, the opposites of the substance. As a result, the substance itself may change.

The third point about illness is that during its course the patient is often provided with a protective shell while the new balance between shadow and substance is being established. This shell can be anything from a day or two in bed with a bout of 'flu, affording a temporary and socially acceptable respite from the pressures of the office, to a much deeper and more permanent shift as happens with a heart attack, a cancer, or a lapse into schizophrenia.

An important function of doctors and other therapists is to sanction this protective shell and thus assist in the establishment of the new balance. Iatrogenic illnesses, that is, illnesses generated by a doctor (through the misuse of drugs for example, through the unfortunate side-effects of drugs, or through the presence of an arrangement whereby a person's well or ill status is pre-determined) may be read as occasions when the exercise of this function is misjudged. In general, the distinction between whether a patient 'chooses' to be ill, or is 'persuaded' to be ill by someone else (relative, friend, or professional adviser) is a fine one. This is particularly apparent in illnesses of a socio-psychological nature, or illnesses in a hyper-dependent patient such as a child.

Parents (under pressure from others such as doctors or teachers) set up models of health for their children who, in turn, absorb these or rebel against them. The complaints the observer meets in a case-study often represent the many aspects of this mixture, the many voices coming from within the individual as well as from the network of individuals in a family or a non-kinship group.

> 'We told him it was only a matter of time before he got ill if he went on working like that every night. But he wouldn't take a blind bit of notice. Now look at the mess he's got himself into'.

> 'What's the trouble? Well, mum says I've got this head-ache'.

The fourth point about illness is that systems of care have become insti-tutionalised; as a result, a lapse into illness tends to be read by a patient and by society not as part of a constant swing between shadow and substance but as a periodic deviation from a state of health. In this sense, the model of illness exemplifies many of the problems noted to occur in other types of deviation: maladjusted as a deviation from adjusted behaviour; eccentric from the norm (see Higgins 1990).

Illness as a whole takes on a stigma; certain illnesses take on more of a stigma than others. How we speak of an illness such as cancer or Aids often betrays fears and phantasies that have little to do with the illness itself (see Sontag 1978 and 1989).

Information Given or Withheld

A student will not need to have advanced far in case-work before realising that patients use the opportunity for voicing their complaints for many different purposes, of which they are often sublimely unaware. Some patients will be able to do the expected: that is, they will be able to pick on a complaint that is troubling them, and to describe it in such a way that the therapist can assist them in easing it.

Unfortunately, many patients are not able to adopt this straightforward approach. They may have difficulty locating the trouble-spot and as a result go round in circles or off at tangents or up blind alleys to avoid getting close to it. They may introduce a number of complaints designed to act as smoke-screens, or to put the therapist off the scent. They may even be dimly aware of what they are doing, and infuriated (or amused) at the confusion they are causing in those responsible for their care.

Some patients may use complaints as a means of holding the therapist in their thrall, or as a mark of status ('I'm schizoid like all great artists') or as a justification for the sorry state they find themselves in.

Another table can be set up, related to the one in Chapter II (p.22):

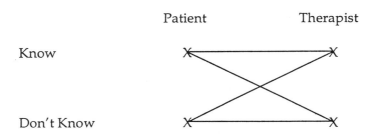

For the conscientious let alone autocratic practitioner, the situation where the patient knows and the therapist doesn't, (implying a withholding of information, or a wavering on the part of patients as to whether they are ready to get 'well') can prove most disturbing. Such patients are described as 'non-compliant'; detailed analyses have been undertaken showing how they can upset the most carefully planned treatment schedules and research designs (see Sackett Haynes and Taylor 1979, Greenberg 1984, Fox 1983 and 1992).

These non-complying patients may sometimes be registering the same sort of protest that any group displays when defined as deviant (albeit they may have accepted society's attitudes and defined themselves as such). The therapist is confronted as the parent who is regulating the patient's health and has to be thwarted accordingly until such time as this image can be modified or discarded.

Once again the central significance of the relation between patient and therapist emerges. On this relation hangs any sense we are to make of the complaints volunteered by the patient. Through Dora and the relation between her and himself, Freud stumbled towards an understanding of what she and he were doing with her complaints. Through a similar relational awareness, the student has to sift the patient's complaints, and grope towards distinguishing what the patient is expecting, consciously and unconsciously, in general, and of the therapist in particular. The exercise cannot be rushed. Changing their mode of complaining, confronting their underlying expectations, is not a transformation over which patients are likely to hurry.

CHAPTER IV

Family History

Biologically and culturally, the family, whether the one from which we spring or the one which we create, provides a central context for all our experience. The context may be calming or abrasive, but it is always there to spark off our responses. We cannot escape the effects of family. Our earliest phantasies, the network of our personal myths, arise out of our responses to the family (whether we confront it, or withdraw from it).

Our responses to the family often entail picking up and re-shaping collective family myths which were around long before we were born and will continue long after we are dead. For the family is the living structure which enshrines past and future generations: ancestors and great-grand-children.

Even if we have no direct kinship links and are orphans, fostered, or adopted, the sense of family still holds us, in some cases even more strongly than if we have well-established blood ties. This sense of family comes about in two ways: through ties to those who stand in for blood relations (such as adoptive or foster parents and their own children, or houseparents and children in a foster home); through an acute awareness, at times, of the absence of blood-ties, seeing others with blood-ties and ourselves without. Adopted children will often go to great pains in adolescence to find their real fathers or mothers, to know where they 'really came from', even though in other respects they are quite content in their adoptive home.

Questions for constructing a family tree

1. *Can the patient (or with the patient's consent a relative) construct a family tree? If so, how many generations on the paternal and maternal side can be traced?*

2. *Can the patient fill in the birth-dates, ages, and death-dates of members on this family tree? Also, how old was the patient when predecessors died and successors were born?*

3. *What were the causes of any deaths?*

4. *What was the nationality, religion, marital status, life-style, occupation, personality, of these different family members? What mental or physical illnesses did anyone suffer from?*

5. *How does the patient relate to these different members on the family tree especially to father and mother, siblings, and their own children? How do the different members relate to each other? How have these relations changed over the years?*

6. *Are there any skeletons in the family cupboard? Alcoholism, suicide, mental instability, epilepsy, abnormal personalities, delinquency?*

Family and Genetics

Recent decades have seen some advance in our knowledge of genetics. This increased understanding of chromosomes, genes, and DNA has a bearing on our behaviour, and on our way of coping with any illness to which we may be pre-disposed. In addition, through this understanding, we are better able to make informed decisions about our own and our children's optimal survival (see further Cookson 1992, Weatherall 1989, Rees 1992, Harper 1992, Chapple 1990).

The establishment of genetic connections, the genotype, in no way automatically explains all aspects of the subsequent response, the phenotype. In the first place, the relation of genes to heredity is a mêlée of hypotheses awaiting falsification. In the second place, from our moment of origin, our responses stem from a combination of genetic endowment with environmental influences. We are a long way from mapping out the degrees of correspondence between the possession of a gene and an overt sequence of behaviour. In an illness such as Huntington's chorea, a correspondence appears to be likely (though even here there is room for variation in the age of onset of the disease, and in its nature and rapidity of deterioration. See Harper 1991). In an illness such as schizophrenia, which may itself not be a single entity, the correspondence is much less clear-cut. If we could establish how the genes operate in this illness, we would still have to examine how these genetic forces link with such socio-psychological forces as 'double binds': those no-win situations that a child has to face when caught in a particular web of parental pressures and category mistakes (Bateson 1973).

Despite these reservations, in taking the family history, inherited patterns, whatever the degree of genetic correspondence, must be of the deepest interest. These patterns may be grouped along a continuum at one end of which are well-established hereditary links such as colour of the eyes, and at the other end much looser links such as a predisposition to use visual rather than auditory imagery, to become depressed, or to vote Tory. In between lie an infinite number of likely links in such features as body-build, temperament, biological rhythms, talents, family affinities and hostilities.

At least three generations should be examined (where at all possible) in any case-study since it is only with this minimal number of generations that we can begin to see the pattern of certain forces, including the skipping of a generation ('She's the spitting image of her grandmother'). The shifting roles in families where sex abuse is a problem sometimes vividly illustrate this three-generational pattern (see Welldon 1988).

Family and Culture

Questions for setting a patient in a cultural background

NB. Family background is one of those sensitive areas referred to in Some Preliminary Questions. It should be broached with tact, the questions often staying in the interviewer's mind rather than being actually voiced.

1. *What are the patient's ethnic roots? How deeply are these accepted? Or rejected?*

2. *How do these roots tally with those of other members on the family tree? Has the family suffered cultural shocks? How long has the family lived in this country?*

3. *What are the patient's religious roots? Is the religion practised actively? Personally? Not at all?*

4. *Again, how do the patient's religious roots tally with those of other member in the family? Is there support or conflict?*

5. *Does the British concept of class (working, middle, and upper) make any sense for the patient and family? Does the patient see the family as slotted into the British class system? Again, is there solidarity, support or conflict? What is the relation of class and caste?*

6. *What are the economic circumstances of the different families in the tree, especially the patient's families of origin and creation?*

7. *What is the atmosphere in the homes of the various family members, but particularly in the patient's home during childhood? What family events occurred during the patient's early years? What outings or family games are remembered?*

8. *What are the social patterns and emotional relationships in the various families but again particularly in the patient's families of origin and creation?*

9. *How could these patterns of family life be represented in a drawing of the family or in plays and stories about it?*

The family transmits a culture in two ways: by the links different family members forge with the outside world through their nationality, religion, occupation, and social life; and by the myriad patterns which are laid down within the family itself, such as kinship systems, the boundaries of a nuclear or extended family, and so on.

No set of questions can hope to cover all these aspects. In taking a history, it is wise and tactful to allow the presentation of family culture to unfold at the pace and along the pathways the patient chooses. The student interviewer, however, may sometimes find it helpful to bear in mind some likely pointers during the unfolding.

How, for example, does the family relate to the outside world? A well-established farming family may enjoy attachments to the local community going back for centuries; family members may continue to play an active part in the running of social and religious events. At the other end of the spectrum, an immigrant family may break not only with its country of origin but also with enclaves of families of similar cultural backgrounds set up in the country of adoption. Infinite variations of family cultural patterns are spun between these two extremes, through changes in national and religious systems, through multiple and mixed marriages, through single parent or substitute families and so forth (see further Qureshi 1992).

Stereotypes (social forces designed to fit us into a particular slot) can play an important part in the make-up of family patterns to which a patient has to respond. One example would be the pressures of class and caste (see Geoff Dyer's contribution on class and literary prejudices in Bradbury and Cooke 1992). We can more easily transcend the restrictions imposed by the class we were born into than those imposed by caste, especially if we stay in the same social climate where caste is a central ingredient. Moving to a climate where caste no longer obtains, we may find it possible to shed the trappings of the caste stereotype but it may take a generation to do so (see further the many articles in anthropological and sociological journals. Also the newspapers of ethnic minorities).

The rules of gender, like those of class, can be defied. Witness Aristophanes' *Lysistrata* and today's feminist movement. A little girl or a grown woman may fight her way out from under a stereotype but neither can escape the limits set by biological facts (rhythmic menstrual changes, a discrete period of life when it is possible to bear a child). Homosexuals and men and women with certain physical handicaps are in analogous socio-biological situations.

From a different viewpoint, the extent to which the family intermeshes with the world around or keeps itself to itself is determined by family policy, which may be deliberately and consciously stated, or implicit and assumed in states of unawareness. Issues of ethnic background, nationality, and religion may contribute to the articulation of this policy but in a pluralist society such contributions may shrink to the marginal. A distinction may be drawn between families who function as relatively closed units, their activities and social relations shared and contained for the most part within the home, and families where the much greater involvement of individual family members with the world outside makes for a much looser structure within the home. The first type of family is often the so-called nuclear family of two generations; the second type is associated with a break-out from nuclearity, including experimental moves such as husband and wife occupying separate menages.

Within the family itself, certain patterns worth noting include:

1. The age-gap between parents (where, for example, in a second or third marriage one parent may be much younger than another); or the age-gap between parents and children where in a late marriage this may be sizeable and in multiple marriages, greatly reduced.

2. The number of siblings and the age-gaps between them, with such issues as being 'crowded out', favouritism, the 'only' child, the burden of twins, the conflation or complementarity of twins.

Despite the presence of common features, it is often the differences between family members that strike both patient and interviewer. These differences in temperament, interests, abilities, often go with conflicts, affinities, and hostilities. We are both drawn to and repelled by someone we sense as being very close to us. These clashes of intimacy are sometimes most vividly illustrated in the history of identical twins, but they can also be very marked in other family relations. The father conceives a particular affection (or hostility) towards the daughter who mirrors and seduces his feminine side. The mother is overwhelmed by the ambiguous feelings she experiences towards a son who reflects her animus.

Some children seem fated to act out a core family pattern. A child may reveal, for example in a schizophrenic breakdown, inherent dishonesties in the parents' marriage. Or a child may assume the role of Rescuer by playing the farceur in an attempt to laugh the family out of a prolonged depression with multiple suicides; or he may indulge in 'shocking' behaviour in an attempt to wake up family members who live their lives half-asleep (see Higgins 1992). On any family tree, this distribution of roles occurs among the parents and children as though they were secretly casting themselves for their specific family play. One aim in taking a family history is to dis-cover these roles.

Family Crises

A family, like an individual, passes through a series of recurrent events which prompt recurrent responses. These landmarks often gather into 'crises', which patients may experience as children in their family of origin, and as adults in the family they create. Sometimes the landmark events may be experienced twice round, as a child and as an adult. In this case, the earlier response is bound to influence the later one for better or for worse (see further the expanding literature on family therapy, e.g. Hodes *et al.* 1991)

These landmarks include:

1. Births and their effects on both parents and children. For the mother, there are the sheer physiological (let alone psychological) stresses of child-bearing, and its immediate aftermath. For the father, there are issues of identification (the couvade) and jealousies. For the children, likewise, problems may well arise over the re-distribution of affection and attention. For the family as a whole, there may be an increased economic burden which at some point may necessitate a change of house.

2. Deaths of grandparents, parents or children. The effects of these on any family member will depend heavily on the age of that member when the death occurred, on how close they felt to the dead one, and on the nature of the death (its suddenness, including suicide or murder, or its painfulness). An important aspect of the patient's response to a death is how deeply he felt (and continues to feel) implicated in it. Children in particular have difficulty sifting their responsibilities, especially when the occasion is shrouded for the child in mystery (non-attendance at the funeral, a veil of silence drawn over all reference to the death, or euphemisms such as 'gone to sleep' or 'passed over').

3. Re-structuring of marital relations: separation, divorce, re-marriage. With one in three marriages in the UK now ending in divorce, this particular landmark in family life with all its consequences may well play a prominent part in patients' experiences. What do we make of the break-up of our parents' marriage? Or of our own? How responsible as children did we feel for the one and as adults for the other? As with death, children may well get muddled over their sense of responsibility for their parents' breaking apart as this is so often fraught, shrouded in secrecy, and may entail tests and battles for allegiance, or the toppling of idols. How parents and children respond to the break-up will influence their response to the consequences of the break-up: the appearance of step-parents and step-siblings; the continuity through 'access' with the original parents and so forth.

For a patient looking beyond these landmarks, there will often be a sense of consistency in family experience, even if this sense of consistency has to incorporate repeated and prolonged doses of chaos. From the family history, both patient and interviewer may be able to outline the growth and the change in the quality of relations between the patient and other family members. Our ties with our parents are never static. We take them inside us (internalise them) and like all the systems we build in this way, what is inside continues to change long after the actual source is gone. The same holds for intimate relations with siblings.

This overall sense of continuity will help to shape adjustments to a family tragedy, such as the birth of a handicapped child, a crippling accident, a chronic illness, loss of employment, imprisonment, infidelities. For besides the ebb and flow of love and hate, of positive and negative evaluations, this overall sense of continuity in family relations includes shifts in what we expect of each other, and in what we expect of ourselves through our interpretation of others' demands. These expectations arise particularly from ties between parents and children. Patients frequently carry expectations in respect of their parents and expectations in respect of their children. Along with these shifts in expectations go changing attitudes towards success, failure, shame and self-esteem.

At adolescence there is often a violent break-away in which the parents are dethroned. The direct effects of this inevitable jump to independence along with the re-shaping of relations that go with it may persist for years. In the course of time, the phase becomes part of the continuity. Many patients, on account of their age alone, will not have reached this state of serenity.

CHAPTER V

The Personal History

Developmental Phases

The landmarks we have explored in the family history have their counterparts in the unfolding of a personal history. For purposes of description, this set of personal history landmarks will be taken as they appear chronologically in the life-chart of the patient. But in practice, of course, they may crop up in no such ordered sequence. A feature of the personal history is often the gap in time which may appear between the occurrence of an event and its subsequent effect. It is as though we live constantly on unexploded time-bombs.

The relation within and between the sequences in human development turns out to be highly complex (see further Harris 1967). In the early phases of developing our sense of self, for example, we hold on to the earlier phase as we move into the next. We may integrate the earlier into the later, but do not abandon this set of earlier experiences. So we arrive at an accumulation of layers, each interacting with the layer above and below (Stern 1985). To a large extent, this accumulation model applies to our development as a whole. The infantile layers become expanded into phases covering our life-span (Erikson 1968).

In addition, however, there is the phenomenon of 'critical period'. If, in one phase, certain changes do not occur, this may mean that they have missed the opportunity to do so and will continue to be absent or deformed for the rest of the patient's life. But since the layers and their parts in the developing system are so inter-twined, this absence or deformation of a particular part may influence profoundly the nature of growth, both in the layer of which it is a part and in the layers that evolve subsequently. There may be attempts, for example, to redress the imbalance by overgrowth (hypertrophy) of parts which up to that point had developed normally. Or the imbalance may spread to involve a much larger portion of the total system.

These critical periods are most in evidence during fetal life when the pace of development is at its height. In the human, gestation may in some ways be conceived as continuing for the first eighteen months after birth, and the time of critical periods may be correspondingly extended. Their full significance is still being investigated.

Foetal life

Questions

1. *What ideas has your patient gathered about his or her conception? Was he or she a wanted baby? If so, for what reasons? Was he expected? Part of a habit? Or was he or she an accident or an after-thought? (Remember how Girolamo Cardano started his autobiography: Before I was born my mother tried to secure an abortion and failed).*

2. *How did gender impinge on parental expectations? Was the patient the long-awaited male heir? Or the female counter-balance to male domination?*

3. *How did other features about the patient satisfy parental wishes? Were these wishes united, or did the father want one feature, the mother another?*

4. *What was family life like during the patient's foetal life? Calm or turbulent? Economic stress?*

5. *How was the mother's health during pregnancy? Did she have any serious illnesses? Raised blood pressure? Did she have to go into hospital for any of these illnesses? Did she have to go in early for her confinement? Was her own or her baby's life ever under threat at any time?*

An irony of case-study is that, as a rule, only the most fleeting information is available on the most crucial phase of a patient's development, the period spent in the womb when the rate of growth is at its maximum. This information is usually based on the accounts the patient received in the past from others, who may or may not have been around at the time and who in any event were relying heavily on their (inevitably selective) memories.

The information about this crucial period is thus subject to at least two layers of distortion: those stemming from the patient's informant(s) and their memory of the events; and those stemming from the patients, and what they remembered the informant saying.

Recently, through various technological advances, new approaches are being introduced. A voluminous literature now exists on the anatomy, physiology, and biochemistry of foetal life and a growing literature on foetal psychological development (see for example Grof in Lewis 1977, Piontelli 1992. For some imaginative sidelights see also Sterne's *Tristram Shandy*). Films that can now be taken of intra-uterine life vividly convey certain events: the persecution of a twin; the withdrawal into thumb-sucking. The increasing extent to which we now have access to the womb and can intervene in foetal development is changing our attitudes towards this early phase. For example, with the possibility of gender and other features now becoming predictable, questions 2 and 3 above take on a rather different significance.

Birth

Questions

1. *What was your physical state at birth? Vigorous healthy and all stations go? Or were there some hang-ups? If so what were these?*

2. *Did you arrive when you were expected or were you premature or late?*

3. *How much did you weigh when you were born?*

4. *How long did labour last? Were there any complications? Unusual position in the birth canal? Breech or limb presentation? Cord round the neck? Born in the caul? Cyanosed or any other signs of foetal distress?*

5. *What was the state of your mother's health after you were born? Did you ever feel responsible for any defects in her health?*

6. *If you think of death as the opposite of birth, how do you conceive of human existence? How does this affect the picture you have of your present illness?*

The sequence of events at birth constitutes one of the most strenuous experiences to which we will ever be exposed. A school of psychoanalysis has sought to make birth trauma and how we coped with it a central feature of our development. While this may seem an overstatement, there is no doubt that the events of birth frequently leave an indelible mark on subsequent development. Some attempt at understanding the nature of any person's birth can be a rewarding exercise in a case-study.

People have attempted to analyse this birth sequence into various phases. Grof, for example, lists in some detail four 'basic perinatal matrices' or sets of experiences occurring in the course of being born. Although these experiences were elicited from patients who were taking LSD at the time, and so clearly may in part be attributable to the drug rather than to the experience of birth, the association of these experiences with memories from post-natal life, with activities in Freudian erogenous zones, and with psychopathological syndromes merits further attention (Grof 1977).

Certainly dim memories of birth events persist and may crop up in dreams and archetypal images. The struggle from darkness into light, the escape from the cave, or the sense of being re-born, are ideas that have gripped us down the centuries. They permeate initiation and Shamanistic rites as well as many religions. In Plato's myth of the cave the passage is reversed. The preoccupation is with what we have left behind rather than with what we are moving towards. But in any event the passage of birth (with death seen as its inverse) puts the whole human journey into perspective.

Recovery from an illness, particularly a psychiatric illness, often has this quality of rebirth. So a patient's familiarity with this archetypal image may bear on the course of his or her return to health.

Infancy

Questions

1. *How was your health during infancy?*

2. *Were there any pointers to areas of the body, or physiological systems, taking precedence over others? (e.g. skin sensitivity, or alimentary or respiratory upsets?)*

3. *Were your biological rhythms quickly established? Or was there a period of instability? In particular, what was your sleep-pattern during infancy?*

4. *What temperamental patterns did you show in your earliest years? How were these different patterns of temperament translated into the expressive gestures of an arts therapy (movement, rhythm, painting, stories)?*

5. *What was the pattern of your early feeding? Were you breast fed and if so for how long?*

6. *How old were you when you sat up? When you walked? How did walking come about? Did you go through a phase of crawling? How soon after walking did you begin to run?*

7. *How old were you when you talked? How did this come about? Did you start with a few groping words? Or, like Bertrand Russell, did you hold back until you burst forth with a long clause-laden proposition?*

8. *Can you remember occasions when you felt painfully and acutely excluded from parental or family intimacies? How did you respond to these occasions?*

9. *Can you remember any periods when you were closely attached to one parent and deeply jealous of the other? How did you resolve these feelings?*

10. *Are you still very close to your parents?*

11. *How have your attitudes to your parents changed down the years as you've discovered things about them and yourself? Have these discoveries increased or decreased your respect for them? Your hostility towards them?*

12. *How far do you find it possible to step into your parents' position and see the world through their eyes?*

In the period of life between birth and about two years, we complete laying the foundation of some central issues in our make-up: the sense of self (personal identity) distinct from other events in the world about us; a sense of trust/distrust in this world; a slow leavening of an instinctive survival ruthlessness with a concern for others.

Some of the work on these issues has been going on during the later phases of foetal life, and it certainly continues long after we have celebrated our second birthday. But the work is particularly intense during these first two years of life outside the womb, the phase called infancy when we are still closely tied to our mother or her substitute. The umbilical cord has only recently been cut and many of us, for varying periods, continue to receive our nourishment and protection from infection through our mother's milk.

For purposes of description, these central issues of infancy have been separated; in practice, the growth of a sense of self, the discovery of the outside world, and the degree of trust in it, the successful integration of concern with ruthless self-interest, all go together. Such inter-relatedness is frequently to be observed in the course of psycho-therapy. We need a sense of self if we are to withstand experiences of being invaded and over-whelmed from without, experiences of chaos, of not being held. Our sense of self, in turn, goes with a sense of personal authority, which involves the exercise of our instinctive drives (our self-preservation and self-love), together with an increasing capacity to control these drives. At first, the control comes, again instinctively, out of some biological sense that a wise parasite has towards the host (a damage limitation formula for not killing off the hand that feeds); then out of some deep love which links us with those closest to us and through them to the world beyond.

In common usage, the word 'selfless' goes with this concern for others, with self-sacrifice. If selflessness is not to be masochistic, it has to be achieved through a genuine integration of the three issues described above.

Various concepts have been introduced to enlarge our understanding of how these central issues become intermeshed. Stern (1985) outlines four phases: the emergent, core, subjective, and verbal selves. Another model concerns an infantile sense of illusion/disillusion associated with 'good-enough' mothering (Winnicott 1965). This model expands the theme of a rhythmic interaction between mother and infant. It suggests that when the rhythms are adequately synchronised, infants experience the satisfaction of instinctive drives (including the satisfactory build-up of tension) as stemming from a benevolent environment. The infant enjoys an illusion of being fused with the environment and of exerting an omnipotent control over it. After repeated occasions when the rhythms are adequately synchronised, infants begin to distinguish a benevolent environment which can be trusted. This trust in the benevolent without is then imaginatively absorbed and lays down a sense of benevolence within (internalisation of the good object).

Conversely, when the rhythm breaks down, the environment is sensed as hostile and persecuting, has to be attacked (spat on, shat on, screamed at, expelled). The sense of self is cut off from what lies about it, and is mobilised into fragments of fury, envy, and hatred.

Everyone's earlier experience contains a mixture of harmonious and dysharmonious rhythms. Winnicott's idea of the good-enough mother postulates a mother/infant relationship where the occasions of harmonious rhythms outnumber those of dysharmonious. Benevolent illusions win out over malevolent disillusions.

Employing different metaphors, other writers have sought to describe this infantile sense of being held or 'dropped', illusioned and disillusioned. Bowlby, drawing on ethnological concepts, speaks of the stages in the infant's 'detachment' from the mother. From an initial position of physical attachment (through the umbilical cord), to that of the autonomous individual in his or her own right, there are many steps involving a sense of loss and replacement.

Others use the idea of 'projective identification', that process in which we split off aspects of ourselves and 'put' them into someone else, who may 'guard' them for us until we are ready to receive them back again into ourselves. (For further explanation see Hinshelwood 1989, Sandler 1988, and Gordon 1965).

Yet another way of describing these central issues of infancy relies on metaphors drawing on visual and dramatic representation: the primal scene; the Oedipus complex. The primal scene metaphor illustrates that moment of truth when infants realise that they are not omnipotent or omnipresent, that they have to endure exclusion from parental intimacies. The scene itself refers to the infant stumbling on the parents when they are engaged in sexual intercourse. But it epitomises the more extended discovery that from early on we have to build our own world and cannot depend on vicarious co-habitation with one or both parents. Reference to the primal scene may be made in a nursery rhyme such as Goosy Goosy Gander, or in various stories where a couple are discovered by a third party in 'flagrante delictu' (for example the scene in the film 'Rainman' where the autistic savant walks innocently into the room where his brother is making love to a girl-friend, and stands watching in bemused curiosity).

The metaphor of the oedipus complex drives home a similar message. Again, the metaphor has sexual roots: the all-embracing attachment of girl infant to father and boy infant to mother, with corresponding murderously jealous feelings towards the parent of the same sex. (The so-called 'reversed' oedipus complex is the name given to the pattern where son becomes attached to the father and seeks to murder the mother; daughter becomes attached to the mother and murderous towards the father.) The metaphor picks up one aspect of the Oedipus story which has provided a fertile ground for dramatists (for example Sophocles' Oedipus trilogy and Shakespeare's Hamlet); it emphasises the identifications we have to live through and transform if we are to achieve sexual authority.

The pace of change during foetal life and infancy is faster than at any successive phase but there is great individual variation. In a case-study it is always important to gauge the pace of change at different phases. In these early years, was the pace faster or slower than normal? Were developmental milestones such as walking or talking passed sooner or later than expected?

The rate of development may be a constitutional feature. Some of us, after all, encompass more than others. But the variation of pace may also indicate such personal characteristics as being in a hurry or being lethargic, being uncomfortable about settling and absorbing situations or being reluctant to get up and go, being greedy for the next experience or feeling replete.

The variation of pace, precocious or retarded responses, may be saying something about parental attitudes to development. Was it the parents who were in a hurry for the child to grow up because they wished to be relieved of the burden of having dependents or because they were pained by having to relive their own childhood through their child?

At all events, these precocious or retarded developments whether in motility, speech, or social relations often have circular, widespread and long-lasting effects.

The Toddler

Questions

1. *How were your statements of defiance delivered? Actively and directly, through saying no or coming up with an opposite suggestion or demand to the one put to you? Or disobeying orders? Or more indirectly through silence or withdrawal?*

2. *How were these statements of defiance coped with by those around you?*

3. *How did you cope with pressure to 'become socialised?' With achieving control over bladder and bowels?*

4. *How did you develop your own imaginative world at any time during early childhood? Did you have secret imaginary friends or relatives? Did you develop this world on your own or in company with an intimate brother, sister, or friend? Did you have a secret language?*

5. *Did you have a special object which had to accompany you wherever you went? How old were you when you became attached to this object? How long did the attachment last? What happened when it got dirty? Were there replacements?*

By the time we are two, most of us are running around busily engaged in building up our own world by discovering the names of things, having conversations with people and, perhaps above all, by making definitive statements. In order to be definitive such statements often have to challenge the comments of those about us. The stage of being a toddler goes with a growing sense of autonomy and this may lead to a heavy use of the word 'No' on the part of toddler and parent alike.

This is the time when we are supposed to start becoming 'socialised', taking control of our bowels and bladder, coping with a younger brother or sister who has an unfortunate tendency to appear at this juncture, and becoming sensitive to slights and humiliations. At this time, we first experience shame.

At this stage too, we are acutely affected by separations as was shown by the Robertsons in their film of a two-year-old going into hospital. Our vulnerability on this score arises from our being in a transition: moving out of the dependence of infancy, we are not yet fully confident in our own person. So the phase of being a toddler has a number of features in common with the phase of adolescence. Both are periods of painful transition and are often accompanied by regressive behaviour which from the consolidated position of adulthood may sometimes bear all the hall-marks of psychosis.

To assist in this transition, the toddler usually finds an object, a bit of the outside world, the Other, with which he is struggling to come to terms. This object may be anything from a doll to a piece of rag. Onto the chosen object are projected an infinite variety of emotions and explorations. The doll/rag or talisman accompanies the toddler into most situations. The two are inseparable, especially at times of falling asleep, when the child has to negotiate the separation from the outside world, the slipping from one level of consciousness to another, the startling appearance of dreams.

This doll/rag is an in-between creature, half-human, half-non-human. It can be endowed with human properties but has the great advantage that any such endowment can be controlled by the toddler. If struck, the doll/rag is capable of as many responses as the toddler chooses to evoke. It can take its punishment meekly, or scream back defiantly.

The doll/rag and its many equivalents, so-called transitional objects, become a central part in any capacity to play. Students in the arts therapies will not be unaware that the various media used as a basis for creative gestures stem directly from these transitional objects.

School and Latency

Questions

1. *How old were you when you started and when you stopped attending school?*

2. *Can you list the schools you went to? What was each one like? How were work and play brought together?*

3. *What aspects of school-life did you enjoy? What subjects, games, clubs were you good at? What did you find difficult or hate?*

4. *What was the pattern of your friendships at school? Did these include teachers?*

5. *Were you ever bullied or teased?*

6. *Were you particularly influenced by any teacher?*

7. *What exams did you pass? Or fail? How did you cope with exams?*

8. *How was your health during your school years? Was your attendance regular? Or were there recurrent or prolonged absences? If so what was the reason for these?*

9. *What attitude did your parents have towards school in general? Towards your schools in particular?*

If all goes well, the lessons and interests at school link with transitional objects. Letters and numbers, albeit in less substantial form, take on the role of the doll/rag. School-games and folk-lore develop the private games. Learning and play fuse.

For students in the arts therapies, the integration of a personal statement with the way such statements have been made down the centuries (a tradition) is an all-too-familiar problem. Yet this is precisely the problem children face when they attempt to relate their private games to more formal traditions embedded in literature or mathematics (reading, writing, and arithmetic).

Just how well these problems are resolved depends in part on the child but also on the climate of a school. The climate may vary not just between schools, but within any particular class in a school at any particular time. What can be gleaned from a case-study is what patients made of their school days: the friendships they formed; the teachers who influenced them; the values they came away with.

Adolescence

Questions

1. *How would you describe your adolescence? As a gradual move into adulthood? Or as a period of turbulent upheavals?*

2. *How did you manage your break-away from home? From the family house or flat? The family mores and values?*

3. *Was the break-away relatively peaceful? Or violently rebellious? What was your parents' attitude to your break-away? What was your attitude to your children when they reached adolescence?*

4. *How did you cope with pubertal changes? The alteration of body shape? The new-found adult genitality?*

5. *How did your sense of identity develop in adolescence? When did you begin to know the direction in which you wanted to go? What attitude did your parents take to this direction?*

6. *Were your decisions about what you wanted to be and do assisted or obstructed by periods of apprenticeship, service in the armed forces and so forth.*

At adolescence, we stand on a threshold and are aware of it. Memories from this time stay with us, often easily retrievable for the rest of our lives. Many of us remain close to adolescence, and continue to see vividly the people and the scenes which pressed in upon us. Because of this closeness, adolescence differs from that other time when we stood on the threshold: the time when we were toddlers and our memories became repressed.

In adolescence, our beliefs and attitudes often assume a stark uncompromising character. Our views are black and white: we have gods and devils, heroes and villains, ideals and anathemas. We are inclined to be extremists: selflessly supporting activities such as VSO (voluntary service overseas), or Greenpeace; or passively retreating into inactivity and isolation. Adolescence is often the time when a schizophrenic breakdown first appears.

Adolescence is punctuated by fundamental physiological changes: spurts in growth, puberty and the move into adult sexuality. These physiological changes are accompanied by psychological and social turbulence. For with the assumption of genital maturity comes the real possibility of rivalling parents: striking out on a course of one's own, finding one's own home, raising one's own family.

For many adolescents, the realisation of this possibility is complicated by a period of studentship, apprenticeship, service in the armed forces and many other types of training. These periods often go with enforced financial stringency and rites of initiation such as qualifying exams.

Being young, vigorous, single, curious, adolescence can easily be a time of frustration, experimentation and rebellion. Different modes of sexuality are often tried out (influenced perhaps by the make-up of institutions in which the adolescent resides). Bizarre flamboyant experiences such as the wearing of novel clothes or hair-styles, or the taking of drugs exert a special appeal.

The Middle Years

Questions

1. *Can you list the jobs you've done? The length of time you stayed in them?*

2. *What took you into them? Was this the result of active choice on your part or were you driven by social and economic pressures, such as your economic status during childhood, the availability of work, parental attitudes to work, education, and training?*

3. *If you have been able to choose a job, what light does this throw on your sense of values? The importance you attach to power, to money, to aesthetic or religious beliefs, to concern for others, or to intellectual curiosity?*

4. *How fulfilled have you felt in your work? What satisfactions has it brought? Where do you see it leading?*

5. *Do you have a steady intimate relation with a person of the same or opposite sex? If so for how long?*

6. *How would you describe it? Good companions? Friends? Lovers?*

7. *Is it formalised in a marriage? With children? (see further in Chapter IV on the family)*

8. *Do you have more than one such relationship going on at present? In the past?*

9. *Do you find the physical side of this relationship satisfying? Does your partner? Are there any points of disagreement between you on this physical side? The nature and frequency of intercourse? Mutual love-play?*

10. *What has been the past pattern of your intimate relations?*

11. *What do you enjoy doing when you're not working? Do you follow these pleasures as much as you'd like to? How do others respond to your following your own pleasures?*

12. *Do you share these spare-time pleasures with your partner or other members of your family?*

13. *Have these activities developed over the years? Or have there been many changes?*

14. Do you have a strong social conscience? If so, how do you exercise it? How does this affect the management of your own life?

15. Do other members of the family share your social conscience and the activities it leads you to undertake?

In the middle years, we are engaged in four pursuits: an occupation which brings in a livelihood; the objects of our sexual desires including marriage and the raising of a family; a social life outside the realms of work, along with hobbies and abiding interests which cannot be pursued whole-time because they are not sufficiently remunerative; social concerns dictated by a social conscience. Examination of any one of these pursuits may reveal deep and characteristic personal patterns in a case-study.

Consider for a moment the work we find ourselves doing. It may result from the economic status of our childhood and adolescence, those years when we were economically dependent on our parents. Given the opportunities in many countries of education and social mobility, the manner in which we cope with economic constraints says much about our character: our determination, initiative, drive, pragmatism, optimism and so forth. Patients may find themselves doing blindly what their fathers and mothers did before them, accepting an occupational mould as though it were inevitable (one aim of treatment may be to provoke patients into questioning such inevitability); or a patient's account of his career may give clear evidence of trying to break out of this mould and of obstructing himself in the process. A woman may refuse to follow her mother's path into being a 'glorified skivvy' but then be overcome by guilt at ceasing to be the 'dutiful daughter'. A man may refuse to follow his father on to the land, or down the mines, or into the services, or into medicine, or into the family business but then falter from a sense of 'letting the side down'.

In so far as we are free to choose a career, the nature of that choice may symbolise fundamental patterns in our character: the bid for power in work along political, administrative, legal or law-enforcing lines; the apparent care and concern in work along social, medical, pedogogic lines. For any individual the symbolic reasons for pursuing a particular line often turn out to be highly complex. Moreover, they may change in the course of a career. Nowadays it is not so unusual for someone to switch directions in the course of his or her working-life: starting out as an artist, for example, and ending as a therapist. Into these complex equations of work choice come such issues as consistency of commitment (with common themes amongst apparent diversity) compensation and over-reaction (the nurse, teacher, doctor whose concern for their charges masks an urge for sadistic control).

The second pursuit of our middle years concerns the elusive and infinitely varied objects of sexual desire. The active forces are related to but different from those determining the choice of work, and contribute to equally fundamental sets of patterns in the case-study.

The mere question of whom we single out as a sexual partner reveals at once the widely ramifying nature of our sexuality: how strong? persistent? sustained? consistent? hetero or homo? numbers of partners? promiscuity? an orgiastic performance? The choice of sexual partners reveals the quality of the relation: sensuous, affectionate, dominant/submissive, sadistic/masochistic? It reveals the nature of our self-esteem and hence personal authority. (The intimacy of sexuality means that the person we make love to becomes, if only momentarily, part of ourselves and hence subject to our own self-evaluation.) The choice of partner reveals the backdrop to our sexual archetypal imagery derived through childhood (our relations to siblings and parents) and infancy. It reveals the boundaries we set up between sexual intimacy and the rest of living. For some, sexuality with sensuality forms a constant undertow in all their experiences. Potential sexual partners, male and female, are all around. Archetypal characters here would be Priapus, or Don Juan. For others, sex is a discrete (and discreet) activity, reserved for one particular person in the secret confines of one particular bedroom. There may be variations in what the sexual act stands for (the confirmation of love, the giving, etc). But the act itself, though a distillation of the infinite ways of relating, is held distinct from these ways it epitomises. The archetypal model here is the Christian conjugal couple.

The choice of sexual partners reveals the changing patterns over time, including the periods of exploration, of raising a family, and of grand-parent quietude.

The relation of work and play for many is quite clear-cut. But in the craft and professional classes especially, the boundaries often become blurred. Burdens of work may be brought home from the office and pursued into the night by a workaholic. Or an artist or writer may never leave home; their work and play merge in their creativity.

The opportunity for contrasting activities (hand balancing brain) and the sharing of such activities with others, in or out of the family, are important areas to cover in the case-study.

Many of us, children, adolescents and adults alike, are very aware of the ever-increasing threats to our continuing existence on this planet. The spread of terrorism, persistent pockets of war, violence and criminal activities, the inner city ghettos, the gaps between rich and poor, the swelling population and diminishing global resources, the background presence of nuclear weapons and the possibility of their proliferation in irresponsible hands, ecological pollution and destruction, global warmings, holes in the ozone layer, these, along with daily accounts of disasters which have happened or are impending, serve as incessant reminders of our vulnerability and fragility. Partly because there is so little we can actually do to modify these threats, most of us practice a degree of cut-off, and focus our attention on what is happening to us rather than on what might happen. We go about our daily business, raise our families, meet our friends, 'cultivate our own garden' as Candide (Voltaire 1759) advised, often the while remaining ironically aware that the ostrich-like quality in this cut-off is an important ingredient in what we and society term 'being sane'.

Patients who break down with a depressive or schizophrenic illness are often unable to sustain Candide's principle. As a prelude or a sequel to their illness, they are preoccupied with different aspects of disasters, which they have either been through (the post-traumatic stress syndrome) or which they are convinced lie ahead.

In any case-study, some measure of social conscience, how we cope with it, how actively we exercise it, and how 'sanely' we keep it in check, is valuable at all ages but particularly during the middle years when we are engaged in shaping the world for our children.

The Third Age

Questions

1. *What are your views about retirement? Do you look forward to it or dread it? If it has happened, how do you experience it?*

2. *What activities do you engage in now that you have retired? Have you started a new career? Or are you rounding out aspects of your old one that you never had time for when you were in full-time work?*

3. *Are these activities solitary or social pursuits? Do you attend evening classes? Or the University of the Third Age? Do you belong to a sports club or any other type of club?*

4. *Do you have a circle of friends? With regular entertaining?*

5. *What has happened to your marriage since you and/or your partner retired?*

6. *What links are you managing to retain with earlier periods in your life? With your past work and work-colleagues? With your childhood and adolescence?*

7. *Do you enjoy solitude? Or companionship? Or both? Have you got the balance right?*

The middle years span the third to fifth decades of our life, from around twenty to around fifty. In many countries, during the past half century, the years from around fifty to around eighty have come to be distinguished as the so-called third age, in contrast to the earlier periods of growth and peak activity (see further Laslett 1990).

This new phase has come about as a result of increasing longevity, improved standards of health, speed of technological change with a corresponding rise in obsolescence, and earlier ages at which people retire or are made redundant. This growing band of senior citizens alters the structure of the society of which they are a part. It presents new opportunities and challenges to society, which has to find means not only of funding their pensions, but also of providing a place in already overstretched social and medical services.

For the case-study, the third age presents yet another threshold following those of the toddler and the adolescent. Unlike the earlier two, the third age threshold has less to do with expansion and get-up-and-go, and more to do with reflection, consolidation, taking stock and rounding out what has been achieved. In this phase, people have the chance to tie up loose ends, to do some of the things they always wanted to do but had no time for while working and raising a family, and to prepare unhurriedly for death.

Often, in this phase, people gain a new confidence. No longer burdened by social restraints such as what their boss will think of them if they do such and such (will I jeopardise my job?), people discover that the third age can be a wonderful time to find themselves.

> When I'm an old woman I shall wear purple
> With a red hat which doesn't go and doesn't suit me
> And I shall spend my pension on brandy and summer gloves
> And Satin sandals and say we've no money for butter...
>
> *(Joseph 1992)*

The changes of direction which are inherent in moving across any threshold do not come without turbulence and even a bout of chaos. Many people are thrown at the prospect and still more the actuality of retirement. The reasons have been well analysed: the break-up of an established routine; lopping off the prestige, status, and social network which went with the job; the new strains on a marriage now that the couple spend the day as well as the night together.

Physical and mental breakdowns are not uncommon around the time of retirement. Sometimes it is as though they have been saved up for this time, rather as minor illnesses may be saved up for the week-end. Marriages, too, are apt to collapse at this time. Partners have time to confront themselves and their relationship without the intervention of 'excuses' (such as a hard day at the office) or 'let-outs' (a week-end work 'conference' at Brighton).

In the third age, there may be an increasing desire for solitude, for coming to terms with oneself, for linking up past phases, for making more out of less, for simplifying and economising one's life, and for non-invasive relations which do not interrupt this solitude. In our culture, such values are not always fully appreciated and retired persons may find themselves pressured into being (artificially) social, buying and doing things they don't want, and generally following the patterns of earlier, competitive days.

Solitude does not come easily in a society where age, quietude and experience tend to be downplayed in favour of youth and the latest idea. Nor does it come easily to people who have relied heavily on others to give their lives significance: parents on the spouse or the children; workers on the institution; a friend on a partner (see further Storr 1988).

Old Age

Questions

1. *How if at all has your life become limited as your years have advanced? Any physical constraints? Special senses? Memory? Orientation?*

2. *Whom can you call on if you fall sick or need some assistance?*

3. *What arrangements have you made for possible increases in dependency?*

4. *Do you still feel you have a great deal to accomplish?*

5. *Are you disgruntled with the world?*

6. *How far are you prepared for death? Are you ready to go? Do you feel fulfilled in life? Do you accept the idea of life being inconclusive, a pervasive sense of what you might have done but haven't?*

7. *Is death seen as an escape? Or an adventure?*

8. *What are your views on the after-life? Or the Day of Judgement?*

9. *What are your views about the persistence of spirit? Or of spirits? Or of the presence of the dead in memories?*

Old age may set in at any time of life. Some children appear and behave like old men or women; some ninety-year-olds retain a child-like sprightliness which rules out any suggestion of senility. Nonetheless, old age comes with the lapping of the years. After eighty, most of us can expect to be and feel in the old age bracket and facing its two major issues: dependency and death.

In a case-study, the measure of old age must include what the patient makes of growing old (do they recognise it? make allowance for it? fight it?) as well as the objective evidence: the drawing in of physical and mental abilities, the slowing of movements, the impairment of the special senses of hearing and sight, the clouding of thought and memories (see further Stuart-Hamilton 1991, Osgood and Sontz 1989).

Coping with old age includes the steps patients take over organising how they are going to be looked after. One of the more painful aspects of old age can lie in the relations between carer and cared for. If the carer resents the sacrifice involved in the care, the old person is as vulnerable as a child handed over to the attentions of a resentful nurse (see further in Godlee 1992, Pritchard 1992). There are some recognised groups where this problem may become particularly acute, where the dependency of old age may set in early: Alzheimer's disease, other neurological diseases, cardio-vascular catastrophes such as strokes and thrombosis, and so on.

The other central concern of old age is how to face death and dying. Some people may reach a sense of fulfilment in their lives and be ready to die. Others may feel deeply unfulfilled and cheated because death has 'come too soon'. How a person copes with death must depend on how constructively he or she has reflected on it. The part death plays in our philosophy of living depends on our conception of what happens outside our earthly existence, on the purpose of our entrances and exits. Many subscribe in some way to a belief in cycles of life, or in the persistence of spirit through memories or through transitional objects such as a sonnet, a sculpture, a temple (see Grolnick and Lengyel 1978). Erikson (1968) sums up the ultimate question of old age as integrity versus despair.

Personality

Questions for mapping the patient's personality

1. *What are some of the comparative measures you or others have taken on your case? Physical measures such as height and weight? Intelligence and learning? Personality traits?*

2. *How would you describe your patient's life-style?*

3. *How is this personal style reflected in the way your patient moves? Or laughs? Or writes? Or draws? Or improvises on a musical instrument? Or plays with words? Or?*

4. *In what way does your patient strike you as unique?*

5. *In what way does your patient strike him or her self as unique?*

Gordon Alport, many years ago, made the distinction between the nomothetic and the unique (Alport 1951). By the nomothetic he meant measures which place a person on a particular scale by comparing his or her performance with that of other members of a defined population. An example of the nomothetic would be measures of intelligence which map people on to a comparative scale: below average, average, and above average.

In assessing personality as unique individuality, we can apply no such comparative scales. Our interest focuses on how an individual uses his intelligence, for example, together with his other faculties in a unique way of coping with the environment. Any particular use and combination rests with that person.

This distinction between nomothetic and unique underlies Alport's definition of personality as the dynamic organisation within the individual of those psycho-physical systems that determine a unique adjustment to the environment. The distinction elaborates a central theme of his book: science and the single-case. It is of crucial relevance to case-study.

The nomothetic measures

The list of nomothetic measures reads like a resume of psychological research. Thus it includes:

PHYSICAL MEASURES

Measures such as height and weight can clearly have a marked influence on people's attitude to the world around them. The dwarf in mythology and in everyday life sees (and is seen by) the world around in a very different light from the giant. In a similar vein, the fat man or woman finds a different slot in the imaginal world from that of the thin man or woman.

All sorts of physical (and physiological) variables may contribute to our world view. Our physique has long been recognised as playing a deeply significant role in our behaviour. Hence the various systems of so-called somato-types: the asthenic, pyknic, athletic types of Kretschmer; the ecto-, meso-, endo-morphic types of Sheldon (see Kretschmer 1949, Sheldon 1940 and 1942).

Certainly in any case-study a rough assessment of somato-type along with any outstanding features of body-build and body-functioning should occupy a central niche. The theatre of our body is, after all, a main arena for self-expression.

MOOD AND TEMPERAMENT

There are many formal scales for measuring different aspects of mood and temperament; therapists may have access to these in the patient's record or decide to apply some of them on their own account. More often a note covering the patient's general appearance, how they move and talk, how they describe their own feelings, and how such descriptions differ from what the therapist observes, will suffice.

Moods are often complex and evanescent. A student should watch for the constancy, perseveration, repetition, or recurrence of a particular mood during the interview; he should note how the mood changes and what prompts the change. Some patients, particularly young children, are often quite open in their display of moods and feelings; others are more guarded, conceal certain moods, or damp down all feelings behind a flat, bland front.

INTELLIGENCE

The therapist may have access to the patient's results on formal intelligence tests such as the Wechsler Scale (the WISC). These can often offer valuable clues to a person's capacity in certain intellectual fields, and reveal discrepancies between ability and performance. The test-results, for example, may suggest that a person is not realising his intellectual capacity, that he is brighter than he believes himself to be. Or vice versa.

So the test-results can sometimes also throw light on the context in which a patient is performing. Is he or she under- or over-stretched?

The different forms in which intelligence is exercised should always be born in mind. The intelligence involved in writing music in strict five-part counterpoint is not the same as the intelligence involved in unravelling a complicated case of fraud. Intelligence, as measured in formal tests, does not necessarily correlate closely with creativity.

The assessment schedules now being used in schools illustrate the various ways of measuring learning ability on nomothetic scales. They register what a child has achieved vis-à-vis an expected (normal) standard and hence the points at which he or she may be failing. In the overall profile of this achievement there may be indications of individuality, but the main purpose of assessment is to provide a comparative picture.

ATTITUDES

Here the various psychological scales diverge into the infinite. To follow a few lines:

1. Assessments of values. How does any person rate the different value-systems he or she meets everyday: power, social, aesthetic, religious, intellectual, economic? How are these value-ratings reflected in the choice of career, of leisure activities (hobbies, second occupation, etc)? How are they reflected in the patient's moral judgements?

2. Attitudes towards an other.

3. Attitudes towards self.

PSYCHOLOGICAL TYPE AND STYLE

Scales for measurement are the psychological equivalents to body-typing. Examples include Jung's system of a two-tiered complementarity between extroversion versus introversion and feeling-sensation versus intuition-cognition (Jung 1946); transactional analytic distinctions of child, adult, and grandparent; Freud's topographical divisions of id, ego, and super-ego, or characterlogical divisions of oral, anal, and genital.

Another approach to distinguishing personalities introduces the concept of style, which derives from our modes of expression. Shapiro describes the 'neurotic' styles of the phobic, hysteric, obsessional, and paranoid (Shapiro 1965). There are also many studies on more specific areas of expression: styles of hand-writing (graphology); speaking and singing; moving.

Indeed, defining style occupies an important place in any of the arts therapies. The choice of what we express (the content), the medium we choose to express it in (visual, auditory, verbal, movement) and how we express it in the medium of our choice (e.g., if visual, whether painting or sculpture, large or small, framed or unframed, coloured or plain), all give clues to our style of the moment, which in turn reflects our style as a whole.

Unique adaptation

The unique person is more than the collection of an infinite variety of scores on an infinite number of nomothetic scales. In addition, the unique may also furnish appearances of elements not yet broken down into any scales. When we think of someone we know (perhaps only remotely) we often light on a characteristic feature which distinguishes him or her from anyone else.

> The way you wear your hat, the way you sip your tea...
> The way your smile just beams... the way you sing off key...

> *(Gershwin 1937)*

Some people are gifted with a talent which causes them to stand out as one in a million. The talent may be anything from athletic ability, a singing voice, vision, intelligence. Or it may be a peculiar mathematical ability such as appears in so called 'idiots savants' or other 'eccentrics'. The life-path of such people is usually determined by this gift and whether they are rewarded or isolated or both depends on what sort of a bargain they can strike with society. On a less dramatic scale, a consideration of gifts and the combination of talents should enter into any case-study, as one approach to identifying the uniqueness that exists in everyone.

CHAPTER VI

Patterns of Progress

Questions about sequential patterns

1. *Can you isolate the main transformations that have occurred in your patient's life? In his or her progress while under your care?*

2. *Can you plot the ups and downs in the onset and progress of the patient's present and previous illnesses?*

3. *Can you describe the link between forward and backward steps in your patient's progress? How have the regressions affected your relationship? What constructive use have you both been able to make of them?*

4. *What have been the main themes in your patient's life and recent progress? What variations have been played on these themes? Have these variations been for the most part minor shifts in a persisting pattern? Or have they included stark contrasts, dramatic upheavals and striking changes of direction?*

5. *What have been the main themes and variations in your relation with the patient?*

6. *Can you detect some of the main polarities which have punctuated your patient's experience? How have these polarities been resolved?*

7. *What opposites or inverses occur to you when you consider your patient's personality, the images cropping up in their dreams or their creative gestures, and your comments on or interpretations of these?*

8. *Can you locate any moments when your patient has confronted an irreconcilable paradox? Was it linked with a double bind in childhood?*

9. *Have you run into paradox in your transference and counter-transference experiences with your patient?*

10. *What instances of mirroring have occurred in your relation with the patient? In the patient's relations generally, that is, with others present and past besides yourself?*

Transformation

As humans we have the capacity to detect and reflect on patterns. Indeed this capacity is perhaps our distinctive human feature. It assumes many forms: the search for invariance in music or maths; the creation of plots; the record of changing patterns in a landscape; the evolution of themes in history. Case-study is a particularly transparent example of an exercise where we seek to map out patterns of change and resistance to change, of transformation and invariance, in an individual and in those closely associated with him or her (including the therapist during the phase of contact and after).

Repeatedly, through this book, aspects of change have been implicit in the questions asked by patient or therapist. Freud's intuition of psycho-analysis as a form of archaeology suggests, through the metaphor of transformation, analogies with more recent studies on the mathematics of cultural change (see Renfrew and Cooke 1979). A referral and a patient's or relative's complaints point to expectations of change, however devious such expectations may prove to be, and however varied the nature of change conceived by the different people who voice the complaint.

A study of family history reveals the ebb and flow between personal and social or ethnological change. Circular patterns of change are constantly at work. We start life with constitutional resources and quickly confront social forces which influence their evolution. Similarly, a personal history illustrates how the different views on what needs to be changed have arisen, and how we go about changing them, realising our talents and responding to our handicaps. A youth who was arrested several times for spraying graffiti wins an award as a mural artist. A man who was nearly burnt to death in the Falklands war becomes a charismatic benefactor.

So transformation informs a case-study in all its aspects. It also insures that case-study is itself subject to this same transcending movement, a point to which I will return in Chapter IX.

Ups and Downs

The progress of any illness can be charted like an economic index: down when it is getting worse and up when it is getting better. When we first slip into illness, and often for the period before we diagnose what is wrong, we are in a down phase. We feel unwell and know that something is wrong. Once we have become aware that something needs to be put right, we have moved into the promising phase of ascent.

In more instances than we realise, our minds and bodies may take care of the illness themselves without recourse to outside intervention. These self-cures do not immediately enter the arena of case-study but they are always worth inquiring about. They may sometimes precede the illness for which eventually outside help is requested.

The pace and nature of the up-phase varies with the accuracy of the diagnosis (by which we mean defining what the illness is all about) and the appropriateness of the treatment. Recovery may be unimpeded, un-complicated, 'uneventful' in medical jargon: an infection responds to – is cleared up by – an anti-biotic: a hysterical paralysis dissolves following a well-focussed interpretation. Not infrequently, bursts of progress alter-nate with relapses. Recovery from a bout of 'flu takes longer than we expected. In psychotherapy it is well recognised that the initial spurt of progress, after an interpretation which is on target, may well be followed by a phase of dis-equilibrium during which the expanded vision brought about by the interpretation is being integrated.

The pace and length of spurts and relapses vary within and between individuals. These periodic shifts are inclined to be swifter and shorter in the young than in the old. But even in terminal illnesses, the slow down-ward tilt is often punctuated by long periods of apparent improvement or plateaux.

Forwards and Backwards

A movement related to ups and downs, and like them worth charting in any case-study, is movement forwards and backwards. In physical and more often in psychological illnesses, we frequently have to retreat to an earlier phase in order to advance. A key to the resolution of a psychological problem lies in the part played by 'regression': the dissolution of long-held sets, habits, and defences, and the re-experiencing of earlier states of mind on an individual (ontological) or species (phylogenetic) level. This re-ex-perience may include the retrieval of lost memories, but it may also involve re-living in a different and more mature setting events which led to our adopting the habits and defences in the first instance. We have to regress if we are to exorcise persistent phantasies and the restrictions they bring in their wake. Regression, going backwards, serves not just our ego but our whole person. It lies at the heart of any creative endeavour.

So, in considering progress, an important task for the therapist is to describe the constructive use to which patients have put their regressions.

Repetition and Variation

A mother escalates the level of suspense in a game with her baby by varying the theme of 'I'm gonna get ya" to 'I'mmmmm gonna get ya'... I'mmmmmm gooooooonaaa getcha'... I'mmmmm gooooooonaaa catcha... 'The variations in the vocalising are accompanied by variations of facial expression, and gestures (Stern 1977).

The infant, from the first few months onwards, may respond in the same principal mode which the mother prefers (in this instance vocalising) or, since the modes have not as yet become differentiated for him, he may respond in a parallel mode by waving arms, kicking legs or smiling. In either event, the central point about the escalation is that it combines repetition with variation.

In repetition we do the same thing over and over again. We establish the familiar. In variation, we set up a persistent theme against shifts and pulls away from it. The persistence of theme behind these shifts and pulls consolidates the experience of the emergent self. Repetition and variation, the recurrence of the theme embroidered, truncated, changed, all confront us with the strange in the familiar, the familiar in the strange. Paradigms for this combination of familiar and strange are Homer's *Odyssey* or Dante's *Divine Comedy:* multifold adventures on a home-bound journey. We learn and expand on the wings of variation but can only do so if anchored in familiar repetition. Developing the strange out of the familiar is counterbalanced by our search for patterns whereby we can process information; the two activities are complementary, although they may involve different systems in the brain (see Pribram 1983).

Once attuned to it, we find theme and variation cropping up in everything we do: in recurrent dreams, in patterns of play, and in behaviour on a short or long time-span (e.g. recidivism). Theme and variation occur across the board in fields of creative activity, in music, in literature, in the shifting presentation of the same image (an icon) in painting, in the kinesic patterns of the dance.

The shifts in variation may be gradual, a slow sea change, a gentle transmutation. They may be simply embellishments of the familiar, adding an extra piece here and there, never really changing the pattern. Some people's lives reflect this minimal change. 'He's just the same as he was forty years ago when I married him' – an ambiguous comment. Is the wife comforted by the solidity, the security of the familiar? Or bored out of her mind by it?

Variation also implies contrast. Each step away from the familiar establishes a way of differing from it. The contrasts of variation introduce explicit ambiguity, the enrichment of possibilities, and the emergence of polarities. In their more extreme forms, the contrasts may result in dramatic turning-points and changes of direction, the outcome of which may be that the theme itself is no longer recognisable.

A case-study may illustrate any type of variation from minor embellishment to contrast-laden upheavals. The variations may become more convoluted as the patient's life unfolds. Or they may fall away and the theme emerge without any decoration. The nature and sequence of our variations reflect key aspects of our personal style. By our mode of variation, we stand revealed.

Symmetry and Inversion

Variations introduce polarities. As Heracleitus pointed out in the fifth century B.C. everything has its potential opposite (an experience that was indelibly imprinted for me by a patient whose disappearance to the Brighton races was always telegraphed by an emphatic denial the day before that he had any intention of going).

This polarisation of opposites implies a symmetry, a balance and the possibility of correcting imbalances. A central plank in Jung's system is the repeated discovery of the opposite or shadow side to any pattern we are consciously registering. From the start of our existence we are engaged in the opposites of differentiation and integration. By the times we are born we have come some way from a symbiotic undifferentiated state, and the evolution of a sense of self as a separate entity (our differentiation) occurs as we begin to attune to and merge with our surrounds (our integration).

Potential inversions are to be found in and around the concept of projective identification. To enumerate a few instances, these inversions may occur between the movements of projection and introjection; between the self and the other into whom or from whom aspects of the self are projected or introjected; between what is esteemed in the self and what is envied in the other; between a ruthless murderous attack on self or other and concerned reparative gestures, which are often accompanied by guilt (see further in Hinshelwood 1989).

An appreciation of opposites underlies our distinction of ourselves as separate entities, the discovery of what is my body and in due course what is me and what is not, our capacity to merge with our surrounds and to transcend our self-boundaries.

One way of defining and relating opposites is to turn things upside down, to invert them. A shy woman dreams she is Winston Churchill, inverting in the dream her waking position, replacing her shyness with bold imperiousness, and her femininity with masculinity. A certain symmetry exists between the dream and her waking experience. By inverting the waking experience in her dream, she moves towards redressing an imbalance. 'I never saw it like that before', a patient may say, on up-ending a phantasy and a whole set of behaviours based on it.

Explore the opposites. In addition to free association, the exercise, while waking or dreaming, of seeking the inverse to any image in a dream often clarifies and sometimes resolves the problems we are facing in the dream. Such constructive and purposeful use of inversion may be found in many studies on lucid dreams and active imagination (e.g. Hillman 1983). The exercise may be extended to any creative gesture: images in a drawing; movements in a dance or musical improvisation; characters and plot in a play. Inversion can provide invaluable new facets to a case-study (see also Johnson 1991).

Paradox

With the emergence of Stern's fourth or 'verbal' self, sometime between the first and second year after birth, an experience which has been with us from the moment we detect the first variation on a theme is thrown into prominence. This experience is that of paradox: the simultaneous irresolvable presentation of two sides of a contradiction.

The capacity to form symbols, of which words are for many the most obvious example, provides us on the one hand with tools of enormous creative power. On the other hand, this capacity confronts us not only with the uncomfortable paradoxical base on which all human experience is founded, but also with potentially severe limitations on our transmodal communications and sixth sense of intuition.

The problem has not escaped a number of workers in the field of depth psychology. Winnicott stressed the paradox lying at the core of the Transitional Object, which should be seen neither as an external object nor as a pure wishful hallucination but as both at the same time. The object is both an object and not an object. It is both out-there and not out-there; both within and not within. Repeatedly, Winnicott stressed the need to embrace this paradox and not attempt to resolve it. To attempt any such resolution, he claimed, was to drop into a Cartesian dualism (Winnicott 1974, Clancier and Kalmanovitch 1987).

Matte-Blanco's representation of the unconscious as infinite sets, where part can represent whole and where contradiction is itself contradicted, is clearly rooted in paradox. So, too, is the bi-logic to which he extends this representation. His so-called Translating Function is based on paradox in that the attempt is made to translate an infinite and symmetrical experience such as a dream or an emotion, into a finite or asymmetrical experience by describing it in words or other symbols (Matte-Blanco 1975).

It is a common experience among those working with families and children that the identification and articulation of a paradox in their behaviour may sometimes suffice to bring about a move from a long-sustained impasse. Winnicott's own case-studies (Winnicott 1971) are full of examples: Robin who goes forwards by going backwards; Ashton who gets excited at the interpretation that his abstract drawings represent simultaneous acceptance and refusal. The experience of paradox may be linked with a double-bind imposed on a patient in childhood, or recapitulated in marriage (Bateson 1973). The Milan School of family therapy focussed their theoretical base on defining the paradox in the family system (Palazzoli et al. 1978). Rycroft's analysis of Miss Y., a case of a paranoid personality, includes repeated references to paradox: a phase in her treatment containing 'two elements which are logically incompatible and which yet co-existed without apparent contradiction': drawings which implied a fear of being too violent 'e.g. very gentle lines on paper that would tear easily'; an attempt to contradict 'anxieties about being a woman and not a man by asserting that her vagina was really a penis' (Rycroft 1985). The emergence of paradox in the transference has been described as the burning cauldron (Savitz 1990).

A young woman patient who had been mute for years once confided to her therapist, 'I can only talk to you if you're not treating me, I mean if you're not the person you are'.

Moments when we confront an irreconcilable paradox are disturbing and explosive. They often mark important junctures in a case, opening up suddenly what has gone before and revealing new connections. Their occurrence is to be treasured.

Mirroring

So far all the processes described in the chapter refer to the person as a separate individual. We can play on our own with themes and variation, inverses, paradoxes. Charts of up and down, backwards and forwards, transformation or turning-points, reflect an individual's progress.

An instance was given, however, of a mother communicating with her infant through one of these processes, variation; in mirroring, or resonating (if an auditory image is preferred), two parties have to be involved. Mirroring is closely related to empathy, mergence, and projective identification. Psychotherapy, Winnicott said, is not about the giving of clever interpretations but about playing back to the patient (mirroring) what the patient brings into the session (Winnicott 1974).

Mirroring enters into all our relations: directly, as when a child imitates a parent or strives to do what he or she thinks the parent wants; or indirectly, when the child fights this pull and strives to do the opposite.

Imitation is a form of mirroring and plays an important part in any learning. But imitation may debase mirroring if it becomes mere copying or is injected with sarcasm, which anyone is quick to detect and find offensive. Imitation by machinery, as in automation, exemplifies this mirroring without sympathy, without the sympathetic interplay of projective identification.

Mirroring is a regular feature of group behaviour. Mirroring takes place in time as well as space, and can work forwards as well as backwards. Strong expectation of an event can sometimes result in a mirroring of it before the event has actually occurred. This may be one explanation of déjà vu. Using mirroring in historical studies may result in the conjuring up of ghosts.

In painting we relate to an object by mirroring it or our feelings about it on paper. In movement therapy the mirroring of movements plays a key part in the mutual experience of them. A four-year-old boy, withdrawn to the point of autism, broadcast with the tapping of his foot a rhythm that more or less followed the pace of his pulse but was eccentric. When the teacher mirrored this rhythm, she found it consisted of alternating 5 and 7 beat bars. Once the child realised his rhythm was being picked up in this fashion, he smiled and started to vary it. A dialogue had begun (see Higgins 1991).

Ultimately, a case-study itself can be seen as an exercise in mirroring. The case-study mirrors living events as sifted through memory and observation; it gives the events a structure which may well not have been apparent at the time they occurred. In this structure, the quality of life-events can also be mirrored in the words with which the writer describes them (see further in Abrams 1953 and Hillman 1990). We will return to this last type of mirroring in Chapter IX.

CHAPTER VII

Formulations

Questions about classification and treatment plans

1. *What is the diagnosis in your case-study?*

2. *What other possible diagnoses have occurred to you?*

3. *On what grounds are you rejecting other possible diagnoses? (differential diagnosis)*

4. *Is your diagnosis based primarily on a classification of medical or of psychological disorders?*

5. *What part in your diagnosis is played by the relation of psyche and soma? How are psychic events affecting somatic and vice versa?*

6. *Are there parallel medical and psychological illnesses in your case-study?*

7. *How are social events influencing your patient's illness? Can the problems be largely attributable to these social events? How has your patient responded in the past to stress? What inner world has the patient built up to cope with stress? What capacity has the patient for play?*

8. *Could there be more than one diagnosis? Multiple illnesses for example? Or more than one level of diagnosis, such as depression arising as a result of post-traumatic stress?*

9. *From your diagnosis can you formulate a treatment plan and can you predict the likely course of the patient's illness including the likely response to the proposed treatment plan (prognosis)?*

Diagnosis, Differential Diagnosis and Prognosis

When we diagnose (make a *diagnosis*), we set an illness in a context. If we diagnose someone as having pneumonia, we set his illness in the context of infectious disease, as distinct from other diseases such as heart disease, cancer, or neurosis. In a case of pneumonia, we expect to be able to isolate an organism which is causing the disease, and which would be susceptible to an appropriate anti-biotic. Diagnosis goes with an appropriate treatment plan.

When we diagnose, we separate out a disease from a range of other possibilities. When we list these other possibilities, we engage in the process of *differential diagnosis*. Along with our diagnosis, there often goes some notion about the course our patient's disease may take, including the response to treatment. If we voice this notion, we are offering a *prognosis*.

The exercise of diagnosis implies a system of definitions and classification. After all, without some such system how could we start separating out one disease from any other? So one advantage of diagnosis is that we relate the new problem which confronts us to similar problems we or colleagues have confronted in the past. When we diagnose, we draw on a traditional body of knowledge and experience; we endow our problem with the time-honoured structures that have arisen out of case-lore.

The danger of diagnosing, with its implicit resort to labelling and systems of classification, lies in the reduction of the unique to an example. The danger lies both in the reduction itself and in the possibility that the example may turn out to be inaccurate. Kokoschka resented being labelled as an Expressionist, partly because he resented being reduced to something that could be labeled at all, and partly because he thought the label 'Expressionist' did not do justice to his art. If he had to be pinned down in this way, he claimed the term Baroque would have been a more just description of his spirit (Kokoschka and Marnau 1992). Similar objections can often be raised over our diagnostic labels (see further in Fulford 1990, Fisher and Levene 1989).

There are three major snags about diagnostic labels. The first is that in defining and classifying entities we often have to work on the assumption that they are discrete and specific, when we know that in fact they are not. The price we pay for arriving at a coherent picture of, for example, a disease or a gene is that we ignore the intricate circular networks in which a disease or gene operates and is operated on. Our coherent pictures have, as a result, a large ingredient of artifact.

The second snag is that a diagnostic label is more likely to carry connotations of illness rather than of health. This is true in particular of psychological labels; terms such as phobia, or depression may describe healthy 'normal' defences (who wouldn't be phobic and depressed at times in our civilised world?), but are usually interpreted as implying a pathological distortion of behaviour. This emphasis on the morbid and deviant assumes a special significance when we remember how easily a diagnostic label may influence future as well as past events (Higgins 1990). 'A diagnosis is indeed a gnosis: a mode of self-knowledge that creates a cosmos in its image' (Hillman 1983).

Third, in imposing too rigidly a system of classification on our data, we may obscure the novel or significant elements. Because features of a patient's illness look like those of a disease with which we are already familiar, it is all to easy to jump to the conclusion that the overall patterns are identical. A man in his mid-sixties complains of increasing lethargy and loss of interest. He has no appetite, is costive, his movements are slow, his posture droops and he never smiles. All these are recognised symptoms of depression. But to equate the symptoms with the disease, to diagnose a case of depression, put the patient on anti-depressants and let the matter rest, would clearly be misguided.

Any of these symptoms might point to a different diagnosis: the drooping posture and expressionless face to Parkinson's disease, taking us into the field of neurology; the loss of appetite and costive bowel to some disorder in the alimentary system; the increasing lethary and withdrawal of interest to a systemic disease such as cancer or to some social catastrophe such as the loss of his job or spouse. Any of these possibilities, if present, might account for the man's feeling depressed; to diagnose depression and ignore these possibilities is to arrive at a lop-sided assessment of the situation.

A diagnostic label, particularly when applied in a psychological frame of reference, often simply serves as a sign-post which guides a phase of search. We engage in a series of diagnoses rather than one. In the example just quoted, we might have been quite correct in first diagnosing depression but, using this diagnosis as a sign-post for further search, we might have gone on to straighten our lop-sided assessment by discovering causes which were leading the patient to feel depressed: for example, that he had some serious underlying illness or that he was mourning his job or wife.

In a psychological frame of reference, the protean nature of diagnosis may be particularly apparent. Terms which are used for childhood disorders cease to be suitable for older age groups; the sheer process of growing up introduces different slants and connotations. The various labels for childhood or adult syndromes are inter-connected: anxiety may accompany obsessions, and both may cover an under-lying psychosis. In the course of a long and successful psychotherapy, it is not unusual for patient and therapist to have run the gamut of psychiatric diagnostic categories.

So the idea of diagnosis as a sign-post with different levels and contexts of search assumes a special significance.

Medical Diagnostic Classifications

Medical classifications follow the systems of the body and the systems of noxious agents which can disturb the body's balance (or homeostasis).

The main systems of the body are:

- neurological (brain, spinal cord, peripheral nerves, sympathetic and para-sympathetic networks);
- special sense organs (eye, ear, nose);
- cardio-vascular (heart, blood-vessels);
- blood (bone-marrow, spleen, cells, plasma);
- the lymphatics (glands and vessels);
- respiratory (upper airways, lungs);
- alimentary (tract and related organs such as liver, pancreas);
- renal (kidneys and urinary tract);
- genital (male and female tracts and organs);
- musculo-skeletal (bones, muscles, connective tissues);
- skin and appendages (hair, nails, teeth);
- endocrines (glands and circulating hormones);

The systems of noxious agents include: infections, poisons, environmental hazards such as air pollution and nuclear radiation.

Medical diagnostic classifications are covered in medical text-books and lie outside the scope of this handbook. (For a useful medical dictionary see Dorland 1988.) But one important consequence flows from the classification of disease by body systems. Enshrined in Western medicine, and based on sound physiological principles, the classification has one inevitable draw-back: the division of the body into these compartments obscures the holistic picture. The practising specialities of medicine, with their separate departments and separate journals, do little to diminish this obscuration.

Our Western medical classificatory system which itself is subject to change over the years (e.g. Richmond 1989) is only one way among many of classifying the body and the diseases it is heir to. Across different cultures and times, other ways have evolved which do not entail the same degree of fragmentation (see, for example, Tauber 1991, Quin 1992).

For a student of case-study, these other ways may be relevant if only because they illustrate a principle that Western doctors sometimes forget: every patient has a personal picture of his or her body and how it operates. These pictures may differ profoundly from the one the medical adviser entertains and this difference can exert a strong influence on the effectiveness of medical treatment. (The setting-up of departments of medical anthropology in Western Europe and America is witness to our growing appreciation of this influence. Cf also the concept of 'compliance' mentioned in Chapter III.) Arts therapists, through their traffic in paintings, movements, rhythms, are often familiar with the personal body-worlds their patients subscribe to. Observations on movements, for example, drawn from dance-movement therapy, may contribute towards a new classification of movement abnormalities in neurology or schizophrenia. Certainly in a case-study, novel ways of classifying the body, its functions and dysfunctions, merit careful analysis.

Classification of Psychological Disorders

Psychological problems do not fall into such clear-cut systems. Their classification has tended towards a more global account and as a result assumes a somewhat loose and untidy look. Categories, as defined by workers in different countries, do not always coincide. A general list of broad headings would include:

- developmental disorders (pervasive and specific) and mental retardation;
- childhood disorders (e.g. disruptive behaviour or non-delinquent conduct disorder, phobias, depression, obsession);
- organic mental disorders (e.g. dementia, drug induced);
- psychotic disorders (e.g. schizophrenia and paranoia);
- mood disorders (e.g. uni- or bi-polar depression);
- neurotic disorders (e.g. anxiety, hysteria, obsessive-compulsive states);

(See further the WHO International Statistical Classification of Diseases Injuries and Causes of death (1987), the so-called ISCD9, and the American Diagnostic Statistical Manual of mental disorders, the so-called DSMIII-R. Also see Spitzer *et al.* 1989).

- personality disorders (or psychopathy).

Looking beyond these syndromes of psychological disorders, increasing attention has been given to other diagnostic contexts which have not always received the attention they warrant in medical classifications (see the growing emphasis on holistic medicine and the growing appreciation of 'adjuvant' psychological therapy in physical illness e.g. Bass 1990, Lovestone and Fahy 1991, Greer *et al.* 1992.)

The first of these contexts is that of psyche-and-soma. Two categories in the DSMIII-R, for example, are eating and sleeping disorders. Eating disorders include conditions such as anorexia nervosa and bulimia; examples of sleep disorders are insomnia, hypersomnia, and the so-called parasomnias such as night-terrors and sleep-walking. But also in this context of psyche-soma are included all the various illnesses that have been labelled psycho-somatic (such as eczema, asthma, epilepsy, rheumatoid arthritis) but that increasingly, as we understand illness, come to be seen as part of a total system rather than as defects of a particular system. There is a constant circular reaction of psyche on soma and vice versa for the simple reason that psyche and soma are obverse sides of the same coin. Parts of the body such as the skin (see Bick 1968, Higgins 1963b), the mouth, the anus, or the musculature, have long been recognised as deeply influencing character structure. In addition, the context of psyche-soma would include the various disturbances of body-image that accompany any illness.

A further diagnostic context in psychological disorders focuses on social forces. Several categories of disorder have been defined where social events figure prominently in the build up of the problems: antisocial responses in childhood or adolescence; academic problems; marital problems; work-problems; bereavement. The syndrome of post-traumatic stress arises ostensibly as a result of some external catastrophe in which the patient is involved. Even here, though, as in the other occasions listed, the distinction between inner and outer events is far from being as clear-cut as the classification might imply. The long-term response to a catastrophe is determined by earlier modes of coping with stress and hence by the different inner worlds we have built up and by our different capacity for play. The same holds for how we cope with problems at work, or in our intimate relations.

The more the patient depends on environmental support, the more likely it is that external events will figure in the diagnosis and the treatment plan. Children are obvious subjects where the part other people play in their lives can assume an over-riding significance (see further on the classification of psychological disorders Szasz 1961, Brown 1991, and Higgins 1990.)

Treatment Plans

Questions

1. *What is your role in the treatment team? Who is responsible for the treatment plan in which you are involved? To whom are you reporting? From whom can you draw support and assistance?*

2. *Is your treatment being carried out in conjunction with other treatments? If so, what arrangements have been made for the co-ordination of these treatments into a coherent plan?*

3. *Do you see your treatment as curing or healing? A remedial exercise or therapy?*

4. *Do others see it in the same light as you do? Or are there discrepancies between what you believe, what you claim to be doing, and what others understand you to be doing?*

5. *How often do you propose to see your patient?*

6. *Do you propose to see your patient individually or in a group? And if in a group, what sort of a group?*

7. *When and in what detail do you propose to acquaint your patient and others (relatives? friends?) with your treatment plan?*

Before embarking on any treatment plan, you need to be quite clear what role you are playing in the team, to whom you should report progress and from whom you can expect support. This treatment network may link with but need not necessarily coincide with the network of referral discussed in Chapter II.

Frequently your treatment forms a part only of an overall treatment plan. As far as possible, you will need to be acquainted with this overall plan and regularly briefed on how it is going. An arts therapy often runs in conjunction with psychotherapy or with a medical regime including the use of psychotropic or other drugs, and with occupational-therapy or physio-therapy. The means for co-ordinating these different parts of the treatment plan should allow for regular joint discussions between those involved. There may be many occasions when experiences drawn from one part of the plan may enlighten, or indeed be essential to, those working in another part (see further Ritson 1989, Murphy 1992).

Various words have been used to define the purpose of treatment in any particular case. There is, for instance, the distinction between 'curing' and 'healing'. Curing evokes the idea of getting back to the state that the patient was in before the lapse into illness. 'Being cured' carries this sense of retrieval of what was lost; disappointment, sometimes litigation, occurs if the retrieval fails to take place or is only partial. Healing, on the other hand, has more to do with transformation. We are concerned less with getting back to the niche we were in before we fell ill, and more with the possibility of expansion, of reaching a place very different from the one we left when we embarked on the healing path.

The term remedial which is often applied to the arts therapies as well as to learning exercises such as remedial reading, inclines us to the cure concept. In remedial exercises patients are given an opportunity to catch up with standards they have failed to meet. Remedial carries an educational, pedagogic flavour. Parents and teachers may feel less threatened if their children or pupils are receiving remedial help rather than therapy.

One major decision in psychological treatment is whether you will be seeing the patient individually or in a group. And if seen in a group, what sort? Kinship or not? Small or large? Open or closed? Reasons for this decision may involve economics as well as therapy. The outcome of the decision will influence many aspects of a case-study, including implications for research design.

A final point about the treatment plan. At some stage (with rare exceptions) you will need to explain to your patients, however young or old, something about what you propose to be doing with them. In some instances, this discussion may amount to outlining a 'contract'. More often it will be an informal briefing, putting the patient (and sometimes friends and relatives) into the picture. Managing this communication effectively may make all the difference in determining the success of your case-study.

Initial and Final Formulations

There are at least two occasions in a case-study, when you should step back and summarise, in your own terms, the position you have reached. The first of these occasions is after the initial interviews when decisions have been taken about a treatment plan. The second and final formulation should be undertaken when you have closed the case.

On both these occasions, you will want to review the complaints and the diagnosis you arrived at, based on these complaints and on your observations of the patient. You may want to sift out the significance of the many different factors contributing to the diagnosis and to the subsequent treatment plan. You may want to check once again how your particular part in the treatment plan fits in to the overall strategy for the patient.

The final formulation provides an opportunity for observing how far the initial formulation has been borne out in practice. Have there emerged discrepancies between earlier and later opinions? Have these discrepancies resulted in a modification of the initial diagnosis, or even a change in it? How have they effected the treatment plan? Has the plan been carried through? Or have there been hitches, which could or could not have been foreseen?

The success of treatment, particularly in psychological disorders, is notoriously hard to assess. This is partly because the time-span of psychological change is usually measured over years. Progressive shifts can occur long after treatment has formally stopped, since (among other reasons) one objective of psychological treatment is that patients learn to conduct their own therapy (the DIY component), and this may take time to prove itself.

There are many discordances, already noted in Chapter III, between surface and hidden attitudes. Mrs A. will emphasise how well she is doing in order to please her therapist, or to get out of the hospital, or because by nature she is an optimist or euphoric. Mrs B. will emphasise how badly she is doing because she fears the nemesis of success ('it'll just get them all jealous') or because she finds it hard to let anyone, including her therapist and herself, feel good, or because her husband will unload all the responsibilities on her again as soon as he thinks she is recovered.

In spite of these obstacles, by holding on to the transformations, however minimal, observed during the course of treatment, by focussing on the effect the patient has had on you during your work together, you will usually find that you can muster some comments on the difference in the situation before and after your intervention. How far this difference can be shown to have anything to do with the intervention itself, how far it can be scientifically recognised as being the effect of your treatment plan, is an issue I address in the next chapter.

CHAPTER VIII

Case-Study and Research

Questions for the setting-up and testing of hypotheses in a case-study
(NB. If the following questions do not immediately make sense because of unfamiliar words, don't worry. As on other occasions, the words are defined in the subsequent text).

1. *In this phase of case-study, are you pre-occupied with understanding the meaning of events? With hearing what the patient says and making some sense of it in terms of his or her world? With translating or playing back the patient's experience? With responding to it as one might to a picture or a piece of music?*

2. *Is this response adequate as an end in itself?*

3. *Or do you harbour a desire to include in the meaning some proof of association between events? Some scientific probing into what goes with what, and what causes what? If so, when?*

4. *What is your hypothesis? And what is the null hypothesis?*

5. *What variables are implied in the hypothesis? Which are the independent and which the dependent variables?*

6. *What is the population referred to in the hypothesis? How do you propose to sample it?*

7. *Could the measures you take of the dependent variable follow a normal distribution and provide you with measures of centrality (e.g. a mean) and spread (e.g. standard deviation)?*

8. *Can you compare two such distributions within or between groups? Is the difference between the two distributions large enough for it to be extremely unlikely that it could have occurred by chance? Does this conclusion falsify the null hypothesis and so leave your hypothesis unrefuted?*

9. *Can you graph a correlation between two or more variables? And derive the correlation coefficient?*

10. *Can you draw regression lines for two or more variables and so map out predictions?*

Meaning and Cause

In case-study we are concerned primarily with disentangling confusions, making sense of the different types of information welling-up from the different layers of consciousness, finding meaning in the complex communications with which we are bombarded when we try to understand another person (see the essay on 'Causes and meaning' in Rycroft 1985).

Our search for meaning can take us in a number of directions, as various people have shown when they start to analyse what meaning means (see Ogden and Richards 1946). We can find ourselves unravelling a sequence of behaviour as though we were translating a foreign tongue. Or we can find ourselves creating new meanings by combining old ones in an imaginative medium. Or we can find ourselves sifting associations, seeing what goes with what, or (if the associations take on a certain sequence) what causes what effect.

If we opt for this last exercise, we may well discover that we are undertaking formal research, where we assess the probability that one event is linked in some way with another. The emphasis in case-study in previous sections has been on the sifting of meaning, which may include eliciting tentative associations or possible causes and effects. Research which is concerned with formally testing such associations and causes grows out of this enquiry into meaning and, in turn, may contribute to the enquiry. But it should always be remembered that there are times (in the arts particularly) when this enquiry into meaning cannot usefully be reduced to the research mould of logical argument and testing of probability statements. Our search for the meaning of an event includes more than our research into its status and significance (see Russell 1932, Bishop 1991).

With this proviso, case-study and research should, on many occasions, go together as complementary moves. Gregory suggests that there are two modes of thinking: the rapid intuitive mode which results in 'hand-waving' explanations; and the slow sequential mode, which he calls 'handle-turning' (Gregory 1992). Along more general lines, Bateson and others have suggested that all advance in creative thought and experience proceeds by the alternation of 'loose' and 'tight' thinking (Bateson 1973). In research we need both the 'hand-waving' loose modes of experience (Medawar's 'imaginative exploit of the single mind') and the 'handle-turning', tight modes (Medawar's testing by experiment, that 'ruthlessly critical process to which many skills and many hands are lent' – see Cooper 1991).

We need our intuitions of case-study to set up hypotheses about which we can then be sceptical. For a basic tenet of the research approach demands that we question every statement that we make. What do we mean exactly by this term or that proposition? Are our definitions, propositions, models, so unambiguous that a fellow researcher knows exactly what we mean? Are our hypotheses so formulated that we or others can prove them false or not?

This mantle of logical scepticism, which we have to put on when we undertake research, can be exciting or disturbing or both. No one finds it easy to have their everyday assumptions questioned and sometimes turned topsy-turvy. Who is going to relish having their more extravagant flights of fancy cut short by prosaic and persistent rational probing? The combination of intuitive flights and their sceptical examination is hard to sustain. That is one reason, an understandable one, why the term 're-search' is apt to pitch students into panic even if they have had some basic scientific training.

But in this respect, research is no different from any other reflexive exercise, familiar to many arts therapy students, such as questioning techniques, classification systems, habits, rituals, or simply why we do this rather than that. The reluctance we often experience over embarking on such exercises may help to explain our reluctance to embark on research.

The remaining reasons for panicking over research are less justifiable. They arise because the student is confused about a number of related basic concepts. These will now be discussed.

Basic Concepts in Research
Variables and hypotheses

The centre of a piece of research is the hypothesis, the statement to confirm which is the object of the research. In a hypothesis, the researcher postulates an association between two or more variables. So to understand what a hypothesis is, we need first to know about a variable.

As the word suggests, a variable is any measure that varies from person to person or object to object, or in the same person or object, over a number of trials. A person's height is a variable. Different people have different heights and a person has different heights at different stages of growth.

An important distinction in variables is whether they are independent or dependent. If we think one variable may have an effect on another, then we carry out an experiment to see whether it does have such an effect. We call the variable that might exert the effect the independent variable, and we call the variable that registers the effect the dependent variable.

If we think that a course of arts therapy sessions has some effect on a person's development, our independent variable would be the course of arts therapy, and our dependent variable some measure of its effects such as improvement of self-esteem, lowering of blood-pressure, enhanced muscle-tone, changes in social responses and so forth. These measures of the dependent variable will be calibrated on various scales such as rating-scores for self-esteem or social response, a chart for blood-pressure, a graph for muscle-tone.

A third type of variable called a hidden or confounding variable is the variable accidentally overlooked when the experiment was set up. Subsequently, in the course of the experiment, the hidden variable is found to be exerting an influence on the results. This influence is separate from but overlaps the influence exerted by our independent variable. A hidden variable thus confounds our results. It renders our experiment invalid. That is, the results we arrive at do not accurately represent the aim we claimed to be testing in our hypothesis.

In research, we attempt to formalise clinical practice into a process in which the patient presents with a problem (the target area), some treatment is given (the intervention or independent variable) and the results of the treatment are assessed (by measures of the dependent variable). The pattern may be summarised as:

Before   Intervention   After

Our objective involves detecting and removing confounding variables in this sequence such as:

1. Bias on the part of the therapist (wanting to prove our treatment effective, wanting our patients to get well).

2. Bias on the part of the patient (wanting to improve, wanting to please or thwart the therapist).

3. False conclusions about causality. The disease may have run its course and the patient be improving before treatment was started. Or improvement may occur under the influence of the therapist's powers of persuasion with no causal relationship to the treatment as such.

The emergence of hidden or confounding variables is one reason why experiments become invalid. Other reasons will surface as we proceed.

In a hypothesis, then, the researcher postulates some association between two or more variables: a course of dance movement therapy sessions (independent variable) enhances muscle tone (dependent variable); drawing a nightmare (independent variable) reduces the level of anxiety aroused by it (dependent variable); group-drumming (independent variable) increases sociability (dependent variable).

In a null hypothesis, the researcher postulates that any such association between two or more variables could have come about by chance. The aim of any experimental research is to test the null hypothesis, that is, to prove or fail to prove that it is false. If the likelihood of the null hypothesis being true can be shown to be remote (a chance of, say, one in a hundred) then we may assume the null hypothesis to be false and, if that is so, we may accept that our hypothesis is valid until a better attempt at dislodging it can be mounted. What research gives us is a body of ideas that stand as yet unrefuted on the grounds of probability. That is the nearest we can get in science to proving them true.

Population and samples

Variables are found in a population, which is a collection or set of people or objects. We might be interested in exploring the effects of an arts therapy (the independent variable again) on a group of old people, or housewives, or accountants, or priests, or toddlers, or married couples, or psychotherapists. In isolating one of these groups in this fashion, we define the population on which we intend to focus our attention.

This definition of a population will appear in our hypothesis, in our null hypothesis, and in our results, and will set clear limits on the problem we are addressing. If our conclusions wander inadvertently beyond these limits, this will be a further source for invalidating our results. For example, we may inappropriately extend our findings to a much larger group than the one we have defined. This criticism has been levelled at attempts to generalise from Freud's limited population of middle-class, late nineteenth century Viennese.

The position is rendered more precarious by the need to sample whatever population we define. It is rarely feasible to include every member of a population we decide to study, even though we have limited that population to a particular group. We could hardly go around testing every clergyman or toddler in the county of Middlesex, let alone the UK or Europe. So we have to settle for a selected sample, following strict rules regarding number and characteristics for our selection. These sampling rules are designed to ensure that our sample is representative of the population we are sampling. Clearly, if our sample is biased in some way, any conclusions we draw from it will be influenced by this bias. We cannot be sure that statements made about a biased sample will hold for statements about the population from which it was drawn. If we can not be sure that the population on which we have based our conclusions accurately reflects the population as defined in our hypothesis, our experiment becomes invalid. Sampling errors are a third source for invalidating experiments.

A population can consist of one person since, as we have seen repeatedly in this book, in any one of us a multitude of collections (populations) are available for testing. Single-case research is the most direct development from a single person case-study. I will return to this type of research shortly.

Frequency and distribution

Variables do not always provide us with the same type of measure. The example given earlier of a person's height is based on a scale made up of positive numbers (120cm, 135.5cm, 135.56987cm etc). We can choose how accurately we wish to record height by deciding on the number of decimal places. (Usually we settle for a scale marked on a ruler.) But the important point is that the scale on which height is based is one where a defined interval (say 15cm.) is the same at any point on the scale where it's selected. The distance between 120cm and 135cm is the same as the distance between 50cm and 65cm. This sort of scale is therefore known as an interval scale.

Two other sorts of scale are the ordinal and the nominal. In an ordinal scale, we can rank our findings in order but we cannot assume that a defined interval is the same throughout the scale. Ordinal scales are often used in psychological measurements, such as intelligence, where we can say that an IQ of 150 is greater than an IQ of 140. But the gap of ten points, say between an IQ of 150 and 140, is not the same as a gap of ten points between an IQ of 110 and 100.

On a nominal scale we are dealing in our measures with categories that are either there or not there, turned on or off like an electric light. Examples: male or female, blue or brown eyed, infected or not infected with typhoid. In this type of measure we can count the number of heads in a population: so many males, so many females. But we cannot fit the results on to any scale, whether with rank orders or intervals.

Each of these three scales requires a different statistical approach when we come to assess the probability of a null hypothesis being false or not.

(For a good introduction to choice of statistical test see Greene and D'Oliveira 1989.)

A key feature of an interval scale is that it often allows us to map our results into a certain type of frequency distribution. That is, we can plot the measures we obtain from our scale (heights, say, from 120cm to 180cm) against the number of people in a population achieving a particular score. In a population of students we can plot how many are 120cm, how many 135cm, how many 150cm and so forth. The resulting pattern of frequency distribution takes the shape of a bell. It is known as the normal distribution.

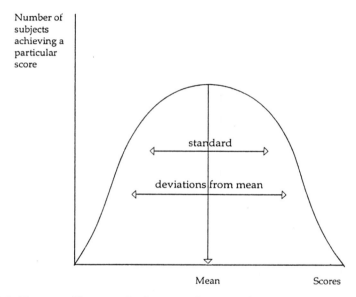

Figure 8.1: Figure to illustrate the features of a Normal Distribution

Univariate analysis

From a normal distribution we can obtain two key measures. The first is a measure of centrality: the height of the bell, the greatest number of people recorded for one particular measure. This particular measure is known as the mean or average. It is calculated by dividing the sum of the scores by the number in the sample.

The second key measure is one of spread from this average peak. Moving symmetrically down the curve on either side of the bell from the peak, this measure of spread is given as so many 'standard deviations' from the mean. A standard deviation is arrived at by another simple formula connecting numbers in the sample with their variance from the mean. A further measure of spread, the standard error, is closely related to the standard deviation, and is used in comparisons of means. (For further details see Swinscow 1990, Hayslett and Murphy 1979.)

Given these measures of centrality and spread, we can now set up an experiment whereby we compare the distribution of one set of results obtained when the independent variable is operating (the test group) with the distribution of another set of results obtained when the independent variable is not operating (the control group). The extent to which the distribution of the test group overlaps that of the control gives us the evidence for believing whether or not the two groups really differ from each other (our hypothesis) or whether this difference could have come about by chance (our null hypothesis).

If the means of the two groups differ by more than a certain amount (say two and a half standard errors) then the likelihood of the difference between the two being due to chance is less than one in a hundred. The null hypothesis is therefore most unlikely to be true, and our hypothesis is therefore upheld.

Multivariate analysis

So far we have considered the distribution of one variable only (univariate analysis). But the same procedure can be followed when we are assessing the differences in distributions between more than one variable (multivariate analysis).

In an experiment on the effectiveness of an arts therapy, we might hypothesise that the therapy enhances muscle tone, *and* reduces the level of anxiety, *and* increases sociability. Our independent variable is again the arts therapy, and our dependent variables are measures of muscle tone, anxiety-level, and sociability. We could compare the difference between test and control groups for the distribution of each of these dependent variables as we did in the case of the single variable. That is, for each dependent variable, we could set up a group where the independent variable was operating (the test group) and one where it was not (the control group). Then we could see if the difference between the two means in our two groups lay more than two and a half standard errors apart.

Methods are available, however, for economising these moves by taking measures of these three dependent variables together rather than separately. In these methods, we analyse the variance not only between test groups and controls, but between the test groups themselves. Through the analysis of variance, we can measure differences within and between the groups we isolate, determine whether such differences are likely to be brought about by chance, and assess how accurately these findings in our sample reflect those to be found in the population from which the sample was drawn.

This analysis of variance is an important tool in research design. But with more than one variable, other possibilities open up. (For further details see Hope 1967 and 1968.)

The correlation coefficient

Suppose we have designed a test which measures certain movement skills. We may want to follow up our design in at least three ways. We may want to see whether someone scoring highly on our test also scores highly on other tests, such as tests for physical ability or intelligence. Do high or low scores on our test go with high or low scores on other tests? Is our test associated with, or related to these other tests?

Or we may want to check the accuracy of our test by seeing whether those who score highly on it win recognition now or in the future for their movement prowess? Is our test an effective measure or predictor of what it claims to be measuring: namely movement skill?

Or we may decide to assess how reliable our test is in the hands of other testers. Do they record scores which tally with ours?

In all these three approaches, what we need is an index of association: between our test and other tests; between our test and some other record of what it purports to measure; between our test, as done on one occasion by ourselves, and its repetition on another occasion by ourselves or by someone else. This index should be some number which indicates whether the association is close, tenuous or non-existent. We call the index a correlation coefficient and arrive at it by using a formula which relates the variance of our two variables.

Where we are searching for the effectiveness of our test, this coefficient will be one of validity. The test is shown to be measuring what we claim it is measuring. Where we are searching for replicability and confirmation of our test by others, the coefficient will be one of reliability.

Correlation patterns and coefficients from the scattergram

Consider the issue of replicability. In assessing a movement sequence, or a musical performance, how sure can we be that experienced therapist A will read and score events along lines that resemble those of another experienced therapist B?

One way of exploring this question would be to show a series of video tapes to A and B, ask them to score a certain item (such as the number of times they noticed a free-flowing movement) on each successive showing of the tape. We could then set out their scores for the series as shown in Table 8.1.

Table 8.1

A	79	43	65	25	72
B	81	42	67	29	68

We translate these scores into a scattergram, with each score from A (recorded along the horizontal x-axis) combined with the corresponding score from B (recorded along the vertical y-axis). So the first score by A of 79, and by B of 81, takes up a single point on the graph. This point has been marked with an arrow in Figure 8.1 to ensure that the translation from Table into graph or scattergram is clear.

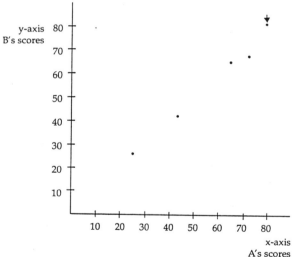

Figure 8.2: The scattergram derived from Table 8.1

We are seeking to measure if and how the two sets of scores, one set from A and one from B, are related. Looking at the graph we are immediately struck by how the points representing the two scores cluster in a pattern running diagonally up and to the right across the page. This particular pattern of cluster reflects a direct association between the two scores, a positive correlation. When we see this pattern, we have confirmed a fairly close tally between the measurements of A and B and we can begin to believe that the two observers are looking at the same events and giving these events closely similar scores.

If ten therapists achieve similar results, we can begin to believe we have a reliable measure. At least among this group!

Of course our experiment might have produced results which could have differed from the above findings in two main ways. We might have found a Table such as Table 8.2:

Table 8.2

A	79	54	33	68	43
B	28	45	62	35	55

And a corresponding scattergram, as appears in Figure 8.2:

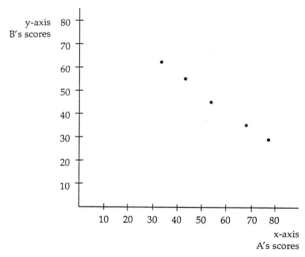

Figure 8.3: Scattergram derived from Table 8.2

Or we might have found a Table such as 8.3:

Table 8.3

A	76	32	.45	50	65
B	52	43	54	72	36

And a corresponding scattergram which looked like Figure 8.3:

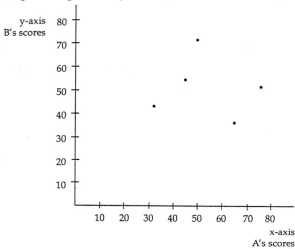

Figure 8.4: Scattergram derived from Table 8.3

In graph 8.2 we see that the points cluster about a diagonal which crosses the page in a direction opposite to that found in graph 8.1. In graph 8.3 we see that the points are scattered higgledy-piggledy over the page, with no line (let alone a diagonal) being suggested in any direction.

Statistically, we can now carry out some analytic moves on these results. By applying our formula for the correlation coefficient, we can obtain a number which measures both the strength and the direction of association between our therapists' records. The number will lie somewhere between 0 and 1 if there is a positive correlation (as in Figure 8.2 where the scores from the two therapists move up and down in the same direction) or between 0 and -1 if there is a negative correlation (as in Figure 8.3 where the higher scores given by one therapist are balanced by lower scores given by the other). The closer the resultant index is to 1 or -1, the stronger the association, positive or negative. The closer it is to 0, the more tenuous the association. In Figure 8.4, the correlation coefficient is virtually nil. So here no association is established between the two sets of scores, and we would have to concede in this eventuality that we have no reliable measure.

Regression lines

When the points appear to be clustering in a particular direction (not necessarily along the diagonal), and regardless of whether positively or negatively inclined, we can take a further statistical step. We can 'fit' a line which follows this direction and which runs as closely as possible to all the points plotted. (For further details see Schroeder *et al.* 1986.) This line we call the regression line because it embodies the mathematical regression of one variable on another (in this case y on x). The regression line has the following valuable properties:

1. A starting point or intercept where it cuts the y-axis. In our example, the intercept would tell us what score observer B might mark up were observer A to register zero.

2. A slope, defined by a number known as the regression coefficient. The slope represents the ratio of the amount of change on the y-axis to the amount of change on the x-axis, and allows us to predict (roughly) the score on the y-axis if we know what it is on the x-axis, and vice versa.

3. A measure of how well the line fits the set of points through which it has been drawn. This measure is called the coefficient of determination and gives us a clue as to how trustworthy is our assumption that there is an association between our variables.

Regression analysis allows for the possibility of deriving more than one association among a number of potential influences. Such a possibility is in keeping with how we often read a situation. For example, in our comparison of observers, we might want to explore what features about them or about the conditions of their observing contribute to the correlation. Does length of experience in movement observation make their results more likely to agree? Does the length of video-strip selected for them to analyse make a difference to the agreement? Or the nature of movements chosen? Or do all three variables, experience, length of video-strip and nature of movements, contribute to the degree of association?

The contributions of these further variables are added to the original equation and new regression coefficients are found. The equation can now no longer be represented by a line on a sheet of paper but by a line in multi-dimensional space with separate slopes for each new variable. These slopes or coefficients indicate the extent of the part played by each variable in the overall pattern of association.

Associations and cause

Through correlations we arrive at associations between two or more variables and through such associations at the underlying structure of possible causes and effects. From what has been said so far, we can begin to envisage how, by the use of correlation and regression, many paths can be slowly traced through a variety of problems and many fields correspondingly mapped out.

One note of warning. Associations between variables do not in themselves necessarily imply a relation of cause and effect. Suppose in exploring the associations with the test on movement skills, one clear positive correlation was established with the possession of a good vocabulary. It would be quite unjustified to assume that one caused the other, let alone to set up a training for increasing vocabulary in the hope that this would improve motile ability. Causality is only one out of four inferences we may draw from the occurrence of an association. The other three possible inferences would be that:

1. The two associated variables are simply caught up with each other, as the rotation of one wheel of a car is caught up with and closely correlated with the rotation of the three other wheels.

2. The two associated variables are related to a third variable. In our movement example, motile dexterity and good vocabulary might reflect a common basis in genetic, or intellectual inheritance.

3. The two variables are associated by coincidence.

Single-Case Research

The basic concepts discussed above may be applied to single-case research. Here the essential model is one we have already met:

Before		After
	Intervention	
The Base-line		New Base-line

In a series of randomised trials the patient acts as his or her own control (as in a within group design) and the results can be submitted to univariate or multivariate analyses.

For example, the design may follow a serial variation: AB, ABA, or ABAB, where A represents the measures taken during the base-line (the period when the independent variable, for example the arts therapy, is *not* operating) and B represents the measures taken during the phase of intervention (the period when the independent variable *is* operating).

These measures may be found to follow a normal distribution, in which case, we compare the distribution during the base-line A (the control set of scores) and the distribution during the phase of intervention B (the test set of scores). We examine the difference between the means of the two distributions and calculate the likelihood of this difference between A and B being significant.

Alternatively, we can search for correlations between events happening during A, or between events happening during B, or between events happening in A as compared with events happening in B.

We can also watch the passage of events in A and B for changes of slope and changes of level. We can apply methods of analysis derived from studies on similar patterns of movement (time-series) such as the fluctuations in regularly recorded economic indices (see further in Kazdin 1982).

The advantages of single-case research is its closeness to clinical practice. The primary purpose of the research is to measure the treatment benefit for the individual along lines that can be tailor-made for this particular person. The research encourages the co-operation between therapist and patient, who can become a co-worker in the research and assist in decisions over flexibility of approach, and variation in levels of rigour. The research provides a direct measure of an individual's (as distinct from a group's) change. As a result, it also provides a basis for co-operative research among therapists comparing these individual differences through systematic replication.

Single-case research also avoids major difficulties, such as recruitment of large numbers, and the cost and management of clinical trials (matching and controls).

The disadvantages of this type of research lie in the limitations imposed on the nature of measurements. One needs to be sure of a stable base-line out of which arise clear-cut changes. These changes should be reversible (back to base-line) and without prolonged carry-over effects. Single-case research is not particularly appropriate for acute or labile problems. A second limitation concerns the nature of controls, particularly the lack of any between-group type of control.

Generalisations in single-case research can only be built up through systematic replication, since each piece of research can only refer to the particular case under scrutiny. But this pattern of generalisation applies to case-lore in general and is a further instance of the closeness between single-case research and clinical practice.

Phases in Research Projects

A central idea of any research project is that it should grow through a number of stages, which may well continue through the rest of our working life (for a useful review of these stages see Harris P 1988 and on a larger scale Reason and Rowan 1981). These stages include:

1. The personal choice of a problem on which to work. This choice will entail initial definition of concepts, model, and hypothesis, that is, the teasing out of meaning. Naturally, these definitions may change as the project develops.

2. The choice is inevitably based on our general interests and experience It may arise in part from our clinical practice, including our case-studies. For many, an important consideration in the early phase of any research project is how it can be related to case-study.

3. The choice of problem will nearly always involve a critical review of the relevant literature. This will help set the project in the context of other work and give some indication whether we are engaged in replication or treading new ground.

4. Once the problem has been identified one possible next step would be a research design based on a single case, which provides its own control.

5. Another possible and alternative next step would be the convening of small groups to discuss various aspects of the problem and so point to possible key areas requiring more formal examination.

6. One route towards generalising conclusions would be the amalgamation of further single case-studies designed along the lines laid out under 4.

7. One type of more formal examination mentioned in 5 would be a controlled survey.

8. Finally, out of the single case-study or group discussion, we may move towards setting up designs for assessing the association of events along research lines established in the physical sciences, that is, including clear definitions of population and sample, of controls and matching, of dependent and independent variables, of reliability and validity in the measuring scales, and of appropriate mathematico-statistical procedures (see further Andersen 1990, Tognoni *et al.* 1991, Smith 1991, Brandon 1991, Herxheimer 1991).

A series of case-studies may valuably be taken, like photographs, at any stage of this research evolution to enlarge, illuminate, and humanise the process.

CHAPTER IX

The Idiom of Case-Study (2)

Questions about the final form of the case-study

1. *Does your case-study hold together as a piece in its own right? Or is it still fragmentary? Too much like a number of disjointed observations collected over an arbitrary period?*

2. *How are some of the basic processes in your case such as transformation or variation translated into the case-study? Does the medium of words in itself reflect these processes?*

3. *Have you used the case-study as you use comments to a patient to convey a liveliness through the medium itself?*

4. *Have you responded with your patient in more than one medium and mode (e.g. in drawing, moving, musical improvisation, as well as in words)? Have you imbued your words with qualities derived from these other media and modes (clarity of vision, richness of ambiguity, etc)?*

5. *How have you dealt with the story-line, i.e., the plot and narration, in your case-study? Can you condense your case-study into an archetypal plot about love, power, mystery with or without a detective type solution?*

6. *How does your case-study stir a catharsis in your reader?*

7. *What points does your case-study have in common with biography, a short-story, a roman à clef? How does it differ from these literary genres?*

8. *What is biographically unique about the person at the centre of your case-study? What is unique about your case-study itself?*

9. *Have you managed to reveal all you wanted to reveal in your case-study? Or have you had to withhold some information in the interests of confidentiality? How has this withholding affected your relation with the patient and the case-study itself?*

More on Transformation: Communication Through the Medium

The transformation of case-study into an art form, like the transformation of a dream into a poem, or the graffiti of the vandal into pop art, entails two related moves: the fashioning of an individual statement into a form that can stir others; and the enlivening of an inert discourse with a spark of individuality (Rapport 1992).

This transformation poses some immediate problems. The first concerns the nature of the artistic impulse. Essential ingredients in an artist's make-up include a gift for playing with a medium, a disciplined training, an urge to fashion a product, and an urge to exhibit it or share it with others. Along with these ingredients often go an overwhelming enthusiasm and a defence against the very feelings which a patient looks to in a therapist. On the face of it, none of these features bodes well for linking therapy with an artistic idiom.

There is an obvious danger that creative preoccupation on the part of the therapist may somehow disturb the attunement with any other person, let alone with a vulnerable subject such as a patient. Nobody except a masochist wants to be someone else's poem or someone else's lover, if that basically means being an instrument for expanding a writer's experience. Who knows what effect subsequent tampering, such as being written up as a case-study or turned into a poem, may have on any therapeutic work?

The problem is well illustrated in Freud's case-studies. The creative spark that enlivens the account of his work with Dora owes not a little to Freud's excitement at his new enlightenment, at his sense of breaking boundaries, not just the boundary between conscious and unconscious, nor the conventional boundary between doctor and patient, but the boundary of the art-form itself in which the events are recorded. Freud as artist-scientist is fascinated at the prospect of transforming the traditions of a medium, the case-study. Papini illustrated this when he imputed to Freud the words: 'I am a scientist by necessity, and not by vocation. I am really by nature an artist...my books in fact more resemble works of imagination than treatises on pathology' (Papini 1969). This fascination inevitably has ambiguous effects on his work with Dora.

Not all therapists are bitten by Freud-the-writer's bug. Many would limit their fascination to the living exchanges which preoccupy them in the phase of transformation their patient is passing through. Good therapy entails the constructive bursting of boundaries in the here-and-now. Why not let it rest there? Why transfer the here-and-now into a record, a written-up case-study? Therapists of this persuasion are totally committed to the exercise in hand and, as they might put it, have no time or desire to dissipate energies in the different exercise of writing up what goes on in a therapeutic exchange. Their case-studies remain their private possession, often with only the barest facts written in their notes.

Whilst there is much to be said for this stance, against it has to be marshalled the inevitability of the creative thrust. The write-up includes reflection, the same sort of reflection that goes on in any creative endeavour (the loose followed by the tight thinking of Bateson). Many creative artists rely on the sense of support which is provided by reflective theoretical under-pinning (see for example Messiaen's tract on his musical language in Messiaen 1944). For these artists, creative energy is not so much dissipated by such under-pinning as generated or at least held by it. The artist creates by pulling together the dry bones of theoretical structure and the unique (and otherwise inarticulate) moments of practice. Both aspects of theory and practice are essential for the work to progress.

In the end the question of transforming case-study into a science or art boils down to whether and to what extent the therapist is caught in a particular transcending purpose. What are patient and therapist prepared to settle for? If the object of the case-study becomes the measure of certain facts, the mapping out of an individual or a social landscape (as described in Chapter VIII), of if the object of the case-study becomes the painting of a picture or the telling of a story in such a way as will move others (as described in this Chapter), then the study merges with larger forms where the nature of conveyance is caught up with the mode of conveying. If we settle for letting the liberating experience of therapy rest with the patient, these larger forms need not concern us. Once we embrace them, however, it would seem important that we avoid recording creative exchanges in a manner that dampens or extinguishes their creative spark.

The writing-up of a case involves transformation from the moment the data are collected. A child does a drawing of a waif who has lost two fingers of the right hand and is watching in terror the approach of an enormous plane. While drawing, she speaks about her fear of being bullied by a boy who is two years younger and much smaller than she is. That was the sum of what came out in the session.

But already the data have undergone several transformations: from some strong hitherto largely inarticulate feelings into a drawing which focusses them; from this visual image into a verbal account of events immediately associated with it; from feeling isolated and unable to confide in anyone into being reminded that there are people around who are sometimes prepared to listen.

Over the course of the next few months, further sets of transformations occurred. It slowly transpired that what really frightened this little girl were not so much the threats from the younger boy as the force of her feelings about what she would like to do to him since, by a process of condensation, he had come to represent everything that had kept her separated from a wayward father. In the build-up of the case-study, then, there was the transformation of outside events into inside feelings; from one symbol into another; from many symbols into one.

Other transformations were occurring in the therapist, who found experiences similar to the child's surfacing from her own past. These parallel sets of transformations enlivened her response to her patient's material and played a significant part in her decision to write-up this material as a case-study. This decision introduced yet a further set of transformations: from a mass of loosely connected observations into an ordered presentation; from an account which was just about comprehensible to the writer into an account which would be fully comprehensible to others; from the inchoate excitement the writer experienced when working with the child into a story which conveyed this excitement to someone coming on the data 'cold'.

Media and Modes

By a medium I mean the channel of sensation and perception we use when we communicate (visual, aural, olfactory, gustatory, tactile, kinaesthetic, and verbal). By modes I mean the different types of communication we develop within these media. In the visual medium, for example, we may communicate by the mode of facial expression, or the mode of drawing, or the mode of sign-language.

There is always an active interplay across media, and across modes within and between media. We frequently combine words with drawings, with facial expression and para-linguistic gestures, sounds, and sign-language. We may draw sounds, or use sounds to convey tastes, scents, touch (e.g. Debussy's Preludes). This interplay stems from our earliest years before we had learnt to distinguish between media, let alone between modes.

In a case-study, particularly in the field of arts therapies, trans-media and trans-modal communication may loom large. A student who was unable to obtain any information about her child patient's family or personal background, was nonetheless able to present a detailed intricate vignette of the child's present experiences through a series of Winnicottian squiggles which she and the child had drawn during the month the treatment lasted. She filled out this visual dialogue with verbal comments but the brunt of the case-study, the force of its impact, was visual rather than verbal.

The same emphasis on a non-verbal medium obtains in many musical or movement presentations. Such case-studies often carry information which is peculiar to the particular non-verbal medium or mode being emphasised and which is lost when we seek to translate it into words. No verbal description of a painting or piece of music can cover quite the same ground as the painting or music itself. The choice of a non-verbal medium in which to express one's emotions or one's style can be a central feature of any case-study.

This is not to argue against the use of words, at any rate in the early stages of writing case-studies. The absence of this crucial verbal dimension in encompassing a case-presentation means a large-scale reduction in areas such as family and personal history, which rely heavily on words. The failure to base a case-study on a verbal medium is equivalent to halting the development of the self before Stern's fourth and culminating verbal phase (Stern 1985).

While the use of words has the disadvantage of obscuring non-verbal expressiveness, their use also has the great advantage of being a medium in which we can catch and reflect qualities from other media and modes. We speak of the writer's eye and ear and in the hands of a good poet, we can dance and sing without leaving our chair. With words we can dissect and clarify experiences in a way that is quite impossible with non-verbal media. Simultaneously with this clarification, indeed as part of it, a new world opens up through the same words:

> Full fathom five thy father lies; Of his bones are coral made;
> Those are pearls that were his eyes; Nothing of him that doth fade
> But doth suffer a sea change
> Into something rich and strange.
> Sea nymphs hourly ring his knell.
> Hark! Now I hear them – ding-dong bell.

> *(Shakespeare W. The Tempest. Act 1. Scene 2)*

The Story-Line

Words are the medium of choice when we want to tell a story. We use them first in piecing events together into a *plot* and then in unfolding this plot discursively in a thousand and one ways, the *narrative*.

The story is the chief means the writer has of engaging the reader's attention. 'The king died *and then* the queen died'. So run the elements of a story according to E.M. Forster, who suggested that arranging events in a time sequence is one way of satisfying our curiosity about what comes next. Another way is to give reasons why things came about in this order. 'The king died and then the queen died *of grief'*. Here we have the basis of plot which enhances a story with causality (see further in Forster 1949). In the imaginative fiction of case-study, the plots often include our theories. Why did a complaint come about? Theories of traumata, primal scene, Oedipal complex. Why did it come about in that form? Theories of repression, or other defences such as splitting. Why did healing come about? Theories of transference and insight. And so on.

This connection between plot and causality bears directly on the issues broached in Chapter VIII. In fiction, we rely on plot to convince us of the causal connection; in research, we resort to proof through probability.

There is more than one type of causal scheme. The question Why? can be answered in terms of time-sequences: what happens first? and what happens after that? Or it can be answered in terms of purpose: what for? To what end? (Teleological cause). Or it can be answered in terms of what archetypal idea, myth, or person is under-pinning the story (formal cause).

All these different types of causality are available for plot. Different writers may favour one rather than another. Freud, for example, favoured the time-sequential type; Jung, the many varieties of formal type.

A plot has usually a beginning, a middle, and an end but the essence of it are the questions: what happens next and how is it connected? On these questions we are carried along to what we sense as an inevitable conclusion. If the plot is tragic, the carriage and conclusion has a cathartic effect on us. We are cleansed and re-born through empathy with another's suffering. If the plot is comic, we experience the same sense of cleansing and re-birth through waves of laughter and relief.

Catharsis is another example of how our experience in plot mirrors that in life (for further on plot see Dipple 1980). Narrative provides the writer with a whole range of such mirrorings. For a start, the different viewpoints that can be selected in a narrative (through whose eyes is the scene being experienced? who is telling the tale?) reflect the constant undertow in case-work, where we are concerned with the building up of subjective and objective worlds (see Chapter II); with the give-and-take between patient and therapist, leading through interpretations (mirrorings) to transformations. The different sets of complaints met in a referral, the different expectations of what the treatment will achieve, the different angles of diagnosis, and the different contributions to the overall treatment strategy are examples of the multiple view-points which the writer has to circumscribe in the case-study narrative (see further on points of view in fiction Lanser 1981).

Any case-study entails one major shift of viewpoint: from before to after a person enters the writer's ken, and that usually means from before to after entering therapy. On crossing this threshold, the original tale with all its earlier scenes and characters is re-fashioned into the therapeutic genre: here begins resistance, transference, and counter-transference. The challenge for the writer is how to bridge this shift in view-point. How do patient and therapist connect the new story with the old? Or resolve the battles which often develop between the two stories?

The sheer variety of viewpoint, the variety of options they offer the writer, is another way in which the narrative mirrors life. As we saw in Chapter VI, variation with its corollary of inversion (shadowing) underpins human development from the moment when infant and mother play with each other. In narrative, the opportunities for theme, variation, and inversion, lie all around. Besides choice of viewpoint, the writer can select for theme and variation from an infinite number of events in the patient's family and personal life, as well as from the infinite modes of treating these: varying the pace, or the focus (close-up or distant, soft or hard), or the tone (ironic, satirical, grotesque, melodramatic). There may be a limited number of types of plot (epic, romantic, struggle for power, mystery, detective, comedy of manners, social realism, etc); there is no limit to how these subjects may be played out.

Just as in real life, past and future constantly punctuate the present, so the writer can punctuate the narrative with flash-backs or flash-forwards. These switches in chronological time can be rendered with varying degrees of discreteness, just as we may have, off the page, greater or lesser awareness of the influence exerted on our present behaviour by memory, desire, and expectation.

Besides selecting from different periods of time, writers can roam in their choice through different levels of consciousness. Here again, they can vary the degree to which they display one level as merging into another (see further the many developments of 'stream of consciousness' writing).

Yet another dimension of narrative involves the question of style. In Chapter V we briefly looked at style as a vehicle for conveying a person's uniqueness. In narrative, style can serve a similar purpose. It can impart a distinctiveness both to the overall effect and to the many parts which go to make up the whole. In *Ulysses,* Joyce purposely varies the literary style of different passages in order to portray the particular people, actions, and ideas involved in each passage and to keep the plot moving forward. In similar vein it is open to the writer of a case-study to tailor the style both to the patient as a whole and to the different themes emerging in the relationship as parts of that whole. One part of the patient may know the soul goes to death in tragedy; another may be living out a picaresque phantasy; a third may be engaged in a heroic comedy of improvement. Each of these different parts may warrant a different style to accompany the different plots.

Features of plot and narrative may be closely linked through transformation. An embryonic link occurs in onomatopoeia, where a word explicitly represents a sound reaching us from the outside world. In this instance the transformation is limited to the sound but there is clearly no reason why the transformation should be restricted to one sense modality. In his *Six Memos for the Milennium* Calvino explores the transformation through words of other senses such as smell and taste. Again there is no reason why we should restrict the transformation to a momentary sensory experience. In his novel *If On a Winter's Night a Traveller,* Calvino explores, through narrative, our experience of incompleted development. Each separate story in the novel breaks off tantalisingly at the point where we become fully engaged with it. The plot which stitches these stories together ends similarly inconclusively.

The overall experiences conveyed by Calvino in these narratives represent very closely a central feature of many case-studies. Exploring these experiences in fiction increases our capacity to explore and write up analogous experiences when they are happening in real life.

In these literary experiments, Calvino broaches another idea highly relevant to case-study: the idea of a frame which 'allows the picture to exist isolating it from the rest, but at the same time recalls and somehow stands for everything that remains outside of the picture'. In a case-study, what remains outside is the un-history, the shadow, whose significance for the inevitable advance of the story-line was weighed briefly in Chapter II (see further a review of Calvino's work in Curtis 1992).

Case-Study and Biography

The literary idiom closest to case-study is biography. For, in both, the elements in the story-line of plot and narrative are anchored in the facts of history. In both, we engage in bridging science and art.

There have been many instances of personality portraits (such as those undertaken by Theophrastus or La Bruyere) which link biography with case-study. But the detailed presentation of an individual's life history only became common practice towards the end of the nineteenth century with the case-histories of Freud and his colleagues. Appropriately enough this was also the time when the biographer took a new turn, shedding many moralistic constraints and assuming a greater detachment and a greater interest in the inner events of the person being delineated (see further Shelston 1977).

Truth as fact and truth as fiction

The biographer is close to the historian. Carlyle went so far as to suggest that history was essentially a series of innumerable biographies. This closeness of history to biography was singled out by writers in the sixteenth and seventeenth century when they began to interpret history as the consequence of human action rather than of divine intervention. This attitude was allied to the search for causes. It stemmed from an interest in why people behave as they do, as well as in what people do.

Biographer and historian are concerned primarily with the truth of fact, as distinct from the novelist, for example, who is concerned with the truth of fiction. The distinction is spelt out in the writings of Henry James, D.H. Lawrence and Virginia Woolf, all of whom were deeply committed to presenting human individuals in hierarchical and kaleidoscopic forms. But the distinction is not clear-cut. The biographer selects, manipulates, interprets, shapes his data. Nowhere is this more apparent than in the vivid impressionism of Aubrey's *Brief Lives,* where the style and the ever-fresh anecdotes are a valuable record of the social and intellectual movements in his Baroque age and, for the reader, it is irrelevant to disentangle fact from fiction.

More recently, a growing appreciation of the circular relation which exists between the mind-set (the inner imaginative world of the explorer) and the environment on to which this mind-set is focussed has further eroded the distinction between fact and fiction (see Mason 1990). In a case-study, where the elicitation of 'facts' depends so heavily on the relation between therapist and patient, and on the tuning-in of the one to the world of the other, the same circular relations exist, (as we saw in Chapter II when examining subjective and objective worlds).

Like the biographer, the writer of a case-study may attempt to sift out the truth of fact, believing this truth to go with inductive and deductive reasoning and a scientific basis: In this sense, as we saw in Chapter VIII, a case-study can contribute to and itself constitute a scientific experiment.

But, again like the biographer, the inevitable selection of facts, and the many different ways of presenting them, leads the writer of a case-study into a region where the truth of fiction cannot be excluded from the truth of fact. In the hands of a researcher alive to the excitement of his subject, the upthrust of the impressionistic line brooks no resistance. Truth as fact merges with truth as fiction, as we have seen in the substance and the telling of Freud's case-histories.

Example

In the past, the purpose of biography was defined as illustrating a moral example. Even the telling of an anecdote was often designed to make a point. North inserted the term 'Noble' into his translation of the title of Plutarch's *Lives*. Boswell's great biography of Johnson was slanted in the same moralistic and adulatory direction. But already, by the seventeenth century, the priorities of the historian were shifting from a moralistic slant in the exemplum to the more agnostic approach of the antiquarian survey. By the time of Lytton Strachey's *Eminent Victorians,* the moral emphasis though still present was quite transformed. The aim was now to 'expose' the patterns of a person as an aspect of an age.

As we saw in Chapter I, the idea of a case-study as an example of a general principle has been central to medical or legal practice. This idea still prevails in those case-studies where what is exemplified is the surface feature of some underlying pattern rather than any moral or ethical judgement.

The case-history thus becomes the microcosm revealing some larger and more generalised issue. But a sea change then takes place in the relation of microcosm to macrocosm. The genre of case-study parallels a development in both the novel and science: an increasing appreciation of the subjective in the objective whether this be streams of consciousness or the fields of relativity.

Instead of quoting a person as an example as a butterfly collector might point to a specimen, the case-study now becomes an end in itself: a roman à clef as Freud put it, that is, a romance whose story and characters contain the key to a real life situation. The story of a microcosm comes to reveal not just some aspect of the macrocosm, but like a hologram, its totality (see Zinkin 1987).

Confidentiality

Victorian biographers concluded that only someone close to the subject of the biography could be trusted to exercise a proper discretion about what personal details may be revealed. The problem thrown up in biography over the public exposure of private lives finds a parallel in case-studies in the issue of confidentiality. The various ploys the biographer resorts to, in respecting personal and family secrets, have a familiar ring for the writer of case-study. But here there is the additional point that the patient did not come to the therapist to be written about but to be healed.

Shelston lists some of the matters for concealment in Victorian commemorative biographies: sexual irregularities, drunkenness, mental instability, religious doubts. In the same ethos, the closer the family tie, the more secure the curtain of discretion.

Nowadays, a different list and a different type of security would prevail. But the disclosing of intimacies still presents the same intractable problem. The patient's confiding in and trusting the therapist lies at the core of all treatment, and the breaking of confidence by revealing, without the patient's permission, identifiable spoken or written details is a betrayal of this trust every bit as great as the indiscreet disclosure by the biographer- friend of Victorian times.

An asymmetry of a kind different from that we encountered in Chapter I creeps into the relation between patient and therapist over the question of what either chooses to reveal about consulting-room intimacies. Patients are free to disclose whatever they wish about their treatment, provided such disclosures are an accurate account. (The laws of libel and slander have to be respected.) Therapists enjoy no such freedom. The sanctions of confidentiality outlined in Chapter I apply *a fortiori* to publication. Any breaking of these sanctions that results in a patient's private and identifiable material becoming public property is unacceptable. It undermines the therapist's integrity, the patient's trust, and the treatment's progress, pro- or retro-spectively.

Genre and Diagnosis

When we considered the implications of diagnosis, reference was made to the power of a diagnostic label to influence the future for patient and therapist alike. The same point applies to the manner in which a case-study is conceived.

'The way we tell our story is the way we form our therapy' (Berry 1982). Patricia Berry's remark carries deep overtones. When we become involved in a plot or a myth, we take on board properties that shape both the perception of events and the writing of them. Our images are our keepers as we are theirs. We see what our ideas, governed by archetypes, allow us to see and record. But this very act of writing in turn shapes our therapy. For example, the stress on narration, the continuity of a story, is essentially the genre of the hero archetype, just as abstraction and reduction (whether to 'libido', or numerology, or a configuration such as a mandala) represent the genre of the old man or senex. In the past different gods would be linked with different genres: gravity with Saturn; speed with Mercury; beauty with Venus; vehemence with Mars. There is no reason to believe that such linking of different genres with different perspectives has lost its force to-day.

Indeed the difference between the attitude we adopt in Chapter VIII (where we traffic in facts, verification, degrees of probability, hypothesis testing) and the attitude outlined in this chapter (where we traffic in imaginative fictions), is perhaps best read as an instance of complementarity between genres. The idea of a transient guiding fiction to provide a purpose for continuing on the way comes very close to the scientific idea of a transient hypothesis which directs our search and which we replace as soon as it is falsified. We need both fictions and hypotheses; we need the times when we live with paradox, as well as the times when paradoxes are temporarily resolved.

Hillman speaks of how we digest events by reflection, the careful collation of what happened: the movement of case-material to subtle matter. 'Therapy requires the fiction of literal realities as the primary material to work on. It must have the raw in order to cook' (Hillman 1983). The cooking involves working up into a plot, the fermentation, mimesis (mirroring) and a mercurial transformation of the original plot into something rich and strange. The gathering and testing of raw material (the shaping and replacement of hypotheses) and the cooking are going on all the time. Each makes the other possible (see further Hunter 1991, Singh 1992).

References

Abrams, M.H. (1953) *The Mirror and the Lamp*. New York: Oxford University Press.

Aldridge, D. (1990) Making and taking health decisions: discussion paper. *Journal of Royal Society of Medicine*, 83, p.720.

Aldridge, D. (1991) Healing and medicine. *Journal of Royal Society of Medicine*, 84, p.516.

Alport, G.W. (1951) *Personality: A Psychological Interpretation*. London: Constable.

Andersen, B. (1990) *Methodological Errors in Medical Research*. Oxford: Blackwell.

Armstrong, D. (1991) *What Do Patients Want?* BMJ 303, 261.

Bass, C. and Murphy, M. (1990) The chronic somatiser and the Government White Paper. *Journal of Royal Society of Medicine*, 83, p.203.

Bass, C. and Murphy, M. (1990) *Somatisation: Physical Symptoms and Psychological Illness*. Oxford: Blackwell Scientific Publications.

Barker, D.J.P., Meade, T.W., Fall, C.H.D., Lee A., Osmund, C., Phipps, K. and Stirling, Y. (1992) *Relation of Foetal and Infant Growth to Plasma Fibrinogen and Factor VII Concentrations in Adult Life*. BMJ 304, 148–52.

Bateson, G. (1973) *Steps to an Ecology of the Mind*. New York: Jason Aronson.

Beckett, S. (1959) *Watt*. p.101–102. New York: Grove Press.

Berry, P. (1982) *Echo's Subtle Body*. Dallas: Spring Publications.

Bick, E. (1968) The experience of skin in early object relations. *International Journal of Psychoanalysis*, 49, 484–6.

Bion, W.R. (1977) *Attention and Interpretation. In Seven Servants*. New York: Jason Aronson.

Bishop, M.G.H. (1991) 'A new cageful of ferrets' – medicine and the 'two cultures' debate of the 1950's. *Journal of Royal Society of Medicine*, 84, 637–8.

Bodley Scott, R. (1965) The bedside manner. *Medical Social Transactions* Vol. 82.

Bradbury, M. and Cooke, J. (1992) *New Writing*. London: Minerva with the British Council.

Brandon, S. (1991) Ethics economics and science. *Journal of Royal Society of Medicine*, 84, 575–7.

Brown, R.G. (1991) Thomas Szasz, mental illness and psychotherapy. *British Journal of Psychotherapy*, 7, 283–294.

Buber, M. (1952) *I and Thou*. Edinburgh: T. and T. Clark.

Casement, P. (1985) *Learning from the Patient. London: Tavistock Publications*.

Chapple, J. (1990) Planning 'new' genetics services. *Journal of Royal Society of Medicine*, 83, 64–5.

Clancier, A. and Kalmanovitch, J. (1987) *Winnicott and Paradox*. London: Routledge.

Clynes, M. (1983) *Music, Brain, and Mind*. New York: Plenum Press.

Cookson, C. (1992) The man who would play god. *Article in the Financial Times* 1.2.92.

Cooper, W. (1991) Peter Medawar. *Article in the Independent Magazine*. 2.11.91.

Cox, M. (1978) *Structuring the Therapeutic Process*. London: Jessica Kingsley Publishers.

Curtis, A. (1992) A treat for the senses: the breadth of Calvino's work. *Financial Times* 1.3.92.

Culyer, A.J. (1991) *The Promise of a Reformed NHS: An Economist's Angle*. BMJ 302, 1253–6.

David, A.S. (1990) On insight and psychosis: discussion paper. *Journal of Royal Society of Medicine*, 83, 325–329.

Dipple, E. (1980) *Plot*. London: Methuen and Co.

Dorland, W.A.N. (1988) *Illustrated Medical Dictionary*. Philadelphia: Saunders.

Erikson, E.H. (1968) *Identity: Youth and Crisis*. London: Faber and Faber.

Feder, E. and Feder, B. (1981) *Expressive Arts Therapies*. Englewood Cliffs, New Jersey: Prentice-Hall.

Fisher, L.A. and Levene, C. (1989) *Planning a Professional Curriculum: Guide to Programme Design*. Alberta: University of Calgary.

Forster, E.M. (1949) *Aspects of the Novel*. London: Edward Arnold.

Fox, W. (1983) *Compliance of Patients and Physicians: Experiences and Lessons from Tuberculosis*. BMJ. 287, 33–5 and 101–5.

Fox, W. (1992) What is the best dose schedule for patients. *Journal of Royal Society of Medicine*, 85, 305.

Frater, A. and Costain, D. (1992) *Any better? Outcome Measures in Medical Audit*. BMJ 304, 519.

Fulford, K.W.M. (1990) *Moral Theory and Medical Practice*. Cambridge: Cambridge University Press.

Gershwin, I. (1937) They can't take that away from me. Song with Gershwin G. New York: Chappell and Co.

Godlee, F. (1992) *Elderly People Abused at Home and in Care*. BMJ 304, 333.

Goffman, E. (1974) *Asylums: Essays on the Social Situation of Mental Patients and Other Inmates*. London: Penguin Books.

Goffman, E. (1984) *Stigma: Notes on the Management of Spoiled Identity*. London: Penguin Books.

Gordon, R. (1965) The concept of projective identification. *Journal of Analytical Psychology*. 10, 127–147.

Green, H. (1992) *Surviving: The Uncollected Writings of Henry Green*. Edited by Matthew Yorke. London: Chatto.

Greene, J. and D'Oliveira, M. (1989) *Learning to Use Statistical Tests in Psychology: A Student's Guide*. Milton Keynes: Open University Press.

Greenberg, R.N. (1984) Overview of patient compliance with medication dosing: a literature review. *Clinical Therapy* 6, 592–9.

Greer, S., Moorey, S., Baruch, J.D.R., Watson, M., Robertson, B.M., Mason, A., Rowden, L., Law, M.G. and Bliss, J.M. (1992) *Adjuvant Psychological Therapy for Patients with Cancer: A Prospective Randomised Trial*. BMJ 304, 675–80.

Gregory, R. (1992) The art of science. (An interview with Christian Tyler) in the *Financial Times* 15/16.2.1992.

Grolnick, S.A. and Lengyel (1978) Etroscan burial symbols and the transitional process. In S.A. Grolnick, L. Barkin and W. Muensterberger (1978) *Between Reality and Fantasy*. New York: Jason Aronson.

Grof, S. (1977) The implications of psychedelic research for anthropology. In Lewis, L. *Symbols and Sentiments: Cross-Cultural Studies in Symbolism*. New York: Academic Press.

Hansen, P.A. (1991) A suggested medical curriculum for learning about complementary medicine. *Journal of Royal Society of Medicine*, 84, 702.

Harper, P.S. (1991) *Huntingdon's Disease*. Philadelphia: Saunders.

Harper, P.S. (1992) *Genetics and Public Health*. BMJ 304, 721.

Harris, D.B. (ed) (1967) *The Concept of Development: An Issue in the Study of Human Behaviour*. Minneapolis: University of Minnesota Press.

Harris, P. (1988) *Designing and Reporting Experiments*. Milton Keynes: Open University Press.

Hayslett, H.T. and Murphy, P. (1979) *Statistics Made Simple.* London: W.H. Allen.

Herxheimer, A. (1991) *Challenge for Clinical Trialists.* BMJ 303, 1076.

Higgins, R. (1963a) Permanence in Institutions. *New Society.* 11.7.63.

Higgins, R. (1963b) The perception of the body surface. *British Journal of Medical Psychology.* 36, 261–270.

Higgins, R. (1963c) The concept of maladjustment: its social consequences. *Human Relations,* 16, 61–73.

Higgins, R. (1990) Emotional and behavioual difficulties: some general points. In Varma, V. (ed) *The Management of Children wih Emotional and Behavioural Difficulties.* London: Routledge.

Higgins, R. (1991) Chapters 11, 12 and 13 on treating the withdrawn child in the use of play, art and music. In Varma, V. (ed) *Truants from Life.* London: David Fulton Publishers.

Higgins, R. (1992) Chapters 1 and 2 on the secret life of the depressed and the neurotic child. In Varma, V. (ed) *The Secret Life of Vulnerable Children.* London: Routledge.

Hillman, J. (1983) *The Healing Fiction.* New York: Station Hill Press.

Hillman, J. (1990) *From Mirror to Window: Curing Psychoanalysis of its Narcissism.* Spring 19, 62–75.

Hinshelwood, R.D. (1989) *A Dictionary of Kleinian Thought.* London: Free Association Books.

Hodes, M., Eisler, I. and Dare, C. (1991) Family therapy for anorexia nervosa in adolescence: a review. *Journal of Royal Society of Medicine,* 84, 359–62.

Hope, K. (1967) *Elementary Statistics: A Workbook.* London: Pergamon Press.

Hope, K. (1968) *Methods of Multivariate Analysis.* London: University of London Press.

Hospers, J. (1967) *Introduction to Philosophical Analysis.* London: Routledge and Kegan Paul.

Hunter, K.M. (1991) *Doctors' Stories: The Narrative Structure of Medical Knowledge.* Princeton: Princeton University Press.

Hutchison, R. and Hunter, D. (1945) *Clinical Methods.* London: Cassell.

Institute of Psychiatry, Department of Psychiatry Teaching Committee. (1982) *Notes on Eliciting and Recording Clinical Information.* London: Oxford University Press.

Johnson, R.A. (1991) *Owning Your Own Shadow: Understanding the Dark Side of the Psyche.* San Francisco: Harper Collins.

Joseph, J. (1992) *Warning.* In Selected Poems. Newcastle Upon Tyne: Bloodaxe Books Ltd.

Jung, C.G. (1946) *Psychological Types or the Psychology of Individuation.* London: Kegan Paul, Trench, Trubner and Co. Ltd.

Kazdin, A.E. (1982) *Single-case Research Designs.* Oxford: Oxford University Press.

Klein, E. (1966) *Etymological Dictionary of the English Language.* New York: Elsevier.

Kokoschka, O. and Marnau, A. (ed) (1992) *Oskar Kokoschka letters 1905–76.* London: Thames and Hudson.

Kretschmer, E. (1949) *Physique and Character: An Investigation of the Nature of Constitution and of the Theory of Temperament.* London: Routledge and Kegan Paul.

Lanser, S.S. (1981) *The Narrative Act.* Princeton, New Jersey: Princeton University Press.

Laslett, P. (1990) *A Fresh Map of Life.* London: Weidenfeld and Nicolson.

Lewis, C.T. and Short, C. (1879) (impression of 1933). *A Latin Dictionary.* Oxford: Clarendon Press.

Lovestone, S. and Fahy, T. (1991) *Psychological Factors in Breast Cancer.* BMJ 302, 1219–20.

Mason, P. (1990) *Deconstructing America: Representation of the Other.* London: Routledge.

Matte-Blanco, I. (1975) *The Unconscious as Infinite Sets.* London: Duckworth.

Mayer, A.C. (1989) Anthropological memories. *Man.* 24, 203–18.

Messiaen, O. (1944) *Technique of my Musical Language.* Translated by Satterfield J. Paris: Leduc.

Mitchell Noon J. (1992) Counselling GP's: the scope and limitations of the medical role in counselling. *Journal of Royal Society of Medicine,* 85, 126.

Moore, T. (1990) *The Planets Within.* Massachusetts: Lindisfarne Press.

Murphy, E. (1992) *Community Care: 'The Cascade of Change'.* BMJ 304, 655.

Ogden, C.K. and Richards, I.A. (1946) *The Meaning of Meaning.* London: Kegan Paul, Trench, Trubner.

Osgood, N.J. and Sontz, A.H.L. (1989) *The Science and Practice of Gerontology.* London: Jessica Kingsley Publishers.

Palazzoli, M.S., Boscolo, L., Cecchini, G. and Prata, G. (1981) *Paradox and Counter-paradox.* London: Jason Aronson.

Papini, G. (1969) A visit to Freud. Reprinted in Rev. *Existential Psychology and Psychiatry* 9.130–4.

Pribram, K.H. (1983) Brain mechanism in music: protegomena for a theory of the meaning of life. In M. Clynes (ed) *Music, Brain and Mind.* New York: Plenum.

Pritchard, J. (1992) *The Abuse of Elderly People: A Handbook for Professionals.* London: Jessica Kingsley Publishers.

Quin, C.E. (1992) The centre thought to control sensory and motor activity in the early history of medicine. *Journal of Royal Society of Medicine,* 85, 102–105.

Qureshi, B. (1992) How to avoid pitfalls in ethnic medical history, examination and diagnosis. *Journal of Royal Society of Medicine* 85, 65–6.

Rapport, N. (1992) Discourse and individuality: Bedouin talk in the Western Desert and the South Sinai. *Anthropology Today.* 8, 18–21.

Reason, P. and Rowan, J. (1981) *Human Inquiry.* Chichester: John Wiley and Sons.

Reason, P., Chase, H.D., Desser, A., Melhuish, C., Morrison, S., Peters, D., Wallstein, D., Webber, V. and Pietroni, P.C. (1992) Towards a clinical framework for collaboration between general and complementary practitioners: discussion paper. *Journal of Royal Society of Medicine,* 85, 161–164.

Redfearn, J.W.T. (1985) *My Self, My Many Selves.* London: Academic Press.

Rees, J. (1992) *Forward Dermatology: Genes Looking for Diseases.* BMJ 304, 590.

Renfrew, C. and Cooke, K.L. (1979) *Transformations: Mathematical Approaches to Cultural Change.* London: Academic Press.

Richmond, C. (1989) *Myalgic Encephalitis, Princess Aurora, and the Wandering Womb.* BMJ 298, 1295–6.

Ritson, B. (1989) *Freer Thinking.* BMJ 298, 1325.

Russell, B. (1932) *Mysticism and Logic.* London: George Allen and Unwin.

Rycroft, C.F. (1968) *A Critical Dictionary of Psycho-analysis.* London: Nelson.

Rycroft, C.F. (1985) *Psychoanalysis and Beyond.* London: Chatto and Windus.

Sacks, O. (1986) *The Man Who Mistook His Wife for a Hat.* London: Pan Books.

Sackett, D., Haynes, R.B. and Tayler, D.W. (1979) *Compliance in Health Care.* Baltimore, M.D.: John Hopkins University Press.

Samuels, A., Shorter, B. and Plaut, F. (1987) *A Critical Dictionary of Jungian Analysis.* London: Routledge and Kegan Paul.

Sandler, J. (1988) *Projection, Identification, and Projective Identification.* London: Karnac.

Savitz, C. (1990) The burning cauldron: transference as paradox. *Journal of Analytic Psychology,* 35, 41–59.

Schroeder, L.D., Sjoquist, D.L. and Stephan, P.E. (1986) *Understanding Regression Analysis.* California: Sage.

Seedhouse, D. (1991) *Liberating Medicine.* Chichester: John Wiley and Sons.

Shapiro, D. (1965) *Neurotic Styles.* New York: Basic Books.

Sheldon, W.H. (1940) *Varieties of Human Physique.* New York: Harper and Bros.

Sheldon, W.H. (1942) *Varieties of Temperament.* New York: Harper and Bros.

Shelston, A. (1977) *Biography.* London: Methuen and Co.

Singh, S.P. (1992) Polarisation of art and science. *Journal of Royal Society of Medicine,* 85, 304.

Smith, R. (1991) *Where is the Wisdom? The Poverty of Medical Evidence.* BMJ 303, 798–9.

Sontag, S. (1978) *Illness as Metaphor.* London: Allen Lane.

Sontag, S. (1989) *Aids and its Metaphors.* London: Allen Lane.

Spitzer, R.L., Gibbon, M., Skodol, A.E., Williams, J.B.W. and First, M.B. (1989) *DSMIII-R Casebook.* Washington: American Psychiatric Press.

Stern, D.N. (1977) *The First Relationship: Infant and Mother.* Glascow and London: Fontana.

Stern, D.N. (1985) *The Interpersonal World of the Infant.* New York: Basic Books.

Storr, A. (1988) *Solitude.* London: Fontana.

Stuart-Hamilton, I. (1991) *The Psychology of Ageing.* London: Jessica Kingsley Publishers.

Stuart-Hamilton, I. (1994a) *A Dictionary of Psychology.* London: Jessica Kingsley Publishers.

Stuart-Hamilton, I. (1994b) *A Dictionary of Cognitive Psychology.* London: Jessica Kingsley Publishers.

Stuart-Hamilton, I. (1994c) *A Dictionary of Developmental Psychology.* London: Jessica Kingsley Publishers.

Swinscow, T.D.V. (1990) *Statistics at Square One.* London: BMA Publication.

Szasz, T. (1961) *The Myth of Mental Illness.* New York: Hoeber.

Tauber, A.I. (1991) On pigeons, physicians, and placebos. *Journal of Royal Society of Medicine,* 84, 328–331.

Tognoni, G., Alli, C., Avanzini, F., Bettelli, G., Colombo, F., Corso, R., Marchioli, R. and Zussino, A. 1991. *Randomised Clinical Trials in General Practice: Lessons from a Failure.* BMJ 303, 969–71.

Varma, V.P. (ed) (1990) *The Management of Children with Emotional and Behavioural Disorders.* London and New York: Routledge.

Voltaire, F-M. A. De (1759) *Candide or Optimism.* Translated by Aldington R. 1928. London: John Lane the Bodley Head.

Weatherall, D. (1989) *Gene Therapy: Getting There Slowly.* BMJ 298, 691–2.

Welldon, E.V. (1988) *Mother, Madonna, Whore.* London: Free Association Books.

Winnicott, D.W. (1965) *The Family and Individual Development.* London: Tavistock Publications.

Winnicott, D.W. (1971) *Therapeutic Consultations in Child Psychiatry.* London: Hogarth Press.

Winnicott, D.W. (1974) *Playing and Reality.* London: Penguin Books.

Zinkin, L. (1987) The hologram as a model for analytical psychology. *Journal of Analytic Psychology,* 32, 1–21.

Index